Sweepstakes
Millionaire

Sweepstakes

Millionaire

How to Win a Life of Luxury
Through Sweepstakes

JOHNATHAN WYKA-WARZECHA

I dedicate this book to anyone and everyone who has ever wanted the thrill of winning a sweepstakes. And after reading this book, my hope is you will win, and win big!

To make sure you get the latest & greatest information on the best sweepstakes out there and winning strategies -- be sure to sign up for our online sweepstakes newsletter at:

http://www.sweeperschoice.com/

Contents

Acknowledgements

I would like to thank both my mother and grandmother, for the numerous hours they listened to me talk about Sweepstakes over the last 9 years. I think both of them have heard a lifetime of information about sweepstakes, and probably more than they ever wanted to know. I'd like to say another thank-you to my mother for the suggestion to put together the sweepstakes software called 'SweepersChoice', without which – it would have never existed.

I'd like to thank several colleagues of mine. Zenon – for listening and probably knowing more than he ever wanted to know about sweepstakes. He had many insights from his years of sales experience at various corporations. David – for offering some interesting marketing insights.

Thank you to the people who agreed to be interviewed in this book: Ken – from SweepsAdvantage, Steve – a fellow who has amazingly won several hundred vacation packages in his lifetime, and Beeb and Roger – whom I met 'digitally' through recommendations of others. Their stories can help give an insight into the world of sweepstakes. Thank you also to Walt for his take on how to win video sweepstakes, and also to Carol McLaughlin, author of the This 'N That Newsletter and the Pennsylvania Sweepstakes Convention organizer. Finally, a big thank-you to the people who agreed to share their winning stories with others! You will find their names sprinkled throughout the book.

A thank you goes out to some of my readers that received an advance copy of this book for helping to do a bit of editing. This includes my mother, my family, sweepers such as Carol & Alberta, and several others. Finally, thank you to one of my readers Ilma, for helping to correct some grammar mistakes.

And finally, of course, I'd like to thank the countless companies who have sponsored sweepstakes to make it possible for people to win amazing prizes. Without their sponsorship, there would be no sweepstakes book, nor any sweepstakes software. Sweepstakes are an excellent way for a company to shine, and this book is a testament to that.

1. Introduction

Hello, my name is Johnathan. I've helped thousands of people win prizes, from everything from books and CDs, to vacation packages, $10,000 cash prizes, $30,000+ sports cars and more.

I decided to put this book together, for several reasons. One, I'd like to help show you how you can increase your chances of winning more, while at the same time benefitting the companies that sponsor them. Two, I've been doing this for almost 5 years, so I learned a lot in that time that I can share with you. I've literally spoken with owners from hundreds of different companies, from Fortune 500 companies, to Mom & Pop shops, as well as hundreds of different people who enter sweepstakes, on a regular

Winners Circle!

"I do consider myself a winner. I started sweeping when I entered a contest on my coupon site. I won a cookbook. I then entered the next contest and won $5,000! I've not won that big again but I do have a well stocked kitchen, (Kitchenaid mixer, Calpholon pans, Cuisineart). My son loves his x-box and guitar signed by Pearl Jam. The craziest win I've had is a mosquito. It really isn't that crazy but it sounds weird. It's actually cut glass and copper wire and is very pretty. I affixed it to a board and framed it, and it hangs in my den. People always comment. My most recent good win is a Howa rifle that I won from On Target magazine." – Sandra D.

basis. My experiences can help show you how to increase your chances of winning, while also helping the companies that give you the chance of winning these amazing prizes. And three, I thought it would be fun!

This book will give you solid strategies on how you can increase your chances and likelihood of winning sweepstakes! Many people have been able to win amazing prizes from a single entry.

This book will also be sharing a number of stories, from myself as well as other sweepers. Some 'sweeping greats' agreed to be interviewed as well -- so you will find their stories here too!

Many of these winners also use SweepersChoice, found here: http://www.sweeperschoice.com/. It is a service that helps people increase their chances of winning more, while saving time to enjoy the prizes they do win. The SweepersChoice service helps to organize sweepstakes for individuals, while helping them enter sweepstakes faster through the built in form filler. It helps to prevent disqualification, because every sweepstakes is entered from their own computer, and they visit every company website page to see the company promotion in order to enter it.

At the same time, we also work with companies to help them benefit from daily exposure within the software, increased newsletter signups, branding, and so forth, which is what they like. We help obtain increased publicity and exposure through our newsletters, forums, and partner websites and companies, so they like working with us, our software, and see a direct benefit from sponsoring a sweepstakes. Furthermore, as of this writing, over 14,000 people read our online newsletter where we give them the latest and greatest information about sweepstakes. (You can sign up too! Just go to http://www.sweeperschoice.com/ , enter your name & e-mail address, and click on the 'Click to Learn More' button). We've had many winners win everything from perfume, makeup to electronics, $1,000 cash prizes – simply from entering the sweepstakes we recommend in our newsletter. Also, from time to time – when someone wins big – we promote those companies through partner newsletters, reaching over 100,000+ people, which is another thing companies like.

I have also included a section at the end of the book geared towards individuals or companies that wish to hold a successful sweepstakes. If you or someone you know within a company wants to run a sweepstakes, please feel free to forward that section of the book to them.

SweepersChoice is designed to be 'win-win-win'. A win-win situation for sweepers, because it helps them save time, and helps them increase their chances of winning significantly. A win-win situation for companies, because they benefit directly from increased word of mouth advertising, branding, exposure, and much more. And finally a win-win situation for the winners, because they just won a prize! ☺

Quick Story – 2012 Atlanta Convention

But, before I really get into the meat of this book, I'd like to share a bit of a funny story. I went to my very first sweepstakes convention in 2012, in Atlanta Georgia. There were about 1000 people going, and I thought it was going to be teaching you how to win more sweepstakes. I thought the majority of people were relatively new to this, and I might be lucky to run into some people who had won $2000-$3000. Those would be the 'big' fish. Boy, was I surprised!

Not only had pretty much every single person there won prizes, but it almost seemed like an unspoken rule that in order to attend you had to have won a minimum of $25,000 or more in your lifetime. There were people who had won 2 to 3 cars, other people who had won jackpots, and other people who had won thousands of dollars worth of electronics. One woman, I think, said she had won 15 big-screen TVs in her lifetime, another usually won 10-15 prizes a month (and for some people, that was considered low) -- and then finally, I was amazed when I heard one gentleman had won over 200 trips in his lifetime. He was one of the speakers. He spoke and shared his story of how he was vacationing with his wife and won another trip because he found an obscure entry form in a bar that appeared to have not been entered by anyone, or at the very least, very few people. And you know what happened? He won a vacation while ON a vacation! How's that for luck?

While most people that enjoy this hobby seemed to be in at least their late 40s, or mid-50s, there were some young people. I ran into this tall blonde girl who was kind of cute, but I think she had just gotten married. (Darn! And actually, I was looking.) But I think she was 26 or 27, and if I remember correctly, she had won a $25,000 car, but she <u>personally</u> felt that she was "brand new" to the world of sweepstaking.

But, it was a very active crowd, a very excited crowd. Some people had known each other for 20 to 25 years, and this was almost like an extended family reunion. Other tables, it seemed just like high school. You have the cool kids, the 'jocks', sitting at one table -- the people that everybody wanted to be associated with -- and of course, these tended to be huge prize winners. Then you had the cliquey fashionable girls in another table (which funny enough, every woman at that table I believe was in her 70s or 80s). But, they were dressed very well. Then of course, you had the intellectuals, who would be doing nothing but talking about strategies how to win more. Evidently jealous of the jocks though. And then finally like any high school, you did have some geeks who just wanted to fit in. They may have not won any "big" prizes -- but they were hoping for that one day when they would get a big win -- and then they would be invited to sit at the "cool kids" table, or at the very least be associated with them.

To top it off, the organizers had made it such that you constantly had chances to win prizes every single day. Every morning they would have a speaker -- but to make sure that people showed up -- they would have prize drawings sometime during the sessions. You never knew when it would happen, but you knew it would. And you would just be hoping that you were one of the prize winners. I personally went to pretty much every session, but because I was a vendor, I missed a few. One night, I had not gotten much sleep, and so slept in and missed part of a session. As luck would have it, apparently that's when I won a big prize. However since I was not there to claim it, someone else did.

Finally, they had many different events that you could participate in, or you could just hang out with friends or make new ones. There were several dinners, a baseball game, plus much more.

Since it was the first time I had gone to Atlanta, I wanted to make sure I did as much as possible. I had the chance to go to the Coca-Cola headquarters, which was rather fascinating. They had the complete history of Coca-Cola in one building, complete with all the advertisements they had run, high-tech gadgets, and it was a fascinating history. I didn't realize that the original inventor of Coca-Cola sold his company to another individual for pennies, who then turned it into the multinational corporation it is today.

I had the chance to go to CNN headquarters, and do the behind-the-scenes tour. There were two different types of tours that one could do, one was the regular tour, and the other was a VIP tour. The VIP tour was expensive, but I thought to myself -- when would be the next time I'm in Atlanta -- and so I decided to do it. And I admit, it was very, very, cool. I got to stand about 20 feet away from some of the newscasters that millions of people saw on television every day. I got to see very well-dressed women going from office to office, and a young kid gawking at how beautiful one of them was. (It was very funny -- there were a lot of men on the tour -- all very serious. And then this young teenager saw this woman, and did a complete 180 as she walked by. What was funny, is that none of the men dared to do that -- maybe some of them were with wives, maybe others felt the women were too beautiful for them – but you could tell that it was something that all of them wanted to do. Everyone laughed, because this boy was pretty much the only one brave enough to do that. And of course, it gave some of the men an excuse to look at the woman, to see what this boy was looking at. But by then, she was already long gone.)

And of course, I hung out with a bunch of different sweepers. I had originally rented a car, but because there were so many people coming to the convention, and I was a bit late to claim my reservation, they had all sold out. Except for one car. A beautiful, bright blue Mustang convertible. It must've been fate. Not only was the color of the car similar to the colors of SweepersChoice, but it would be a lot of fun to drive. And I got to share this with a bunch of different sweepers who really enjoy going from place to place with the top down. (And I admit, another one of the sweepers had a very cute daughter that went there with her, and we seemed to get along great -- but she had a boyfriend! Darn again!)

And finally, I also got a chance to speak with the girl from Roboform. We had a very interesting discussion, and discussed the possibility of working together, to help give sweepers more chances winning, while also benefiting the sponsors that provided the prizes.

So all in all, it was very interesting experience. I did not realize just how passionate some of these people were about winning prizes, but I could tell that most people loved it. Whether it was the first win they had ever had in their life that got them hooked, or they just liked the new friendships they made -- there were a lot of happy people.

2013 Utah Sweepstakes Convention

The 2013 Utah sweepstakes convention was a very interesting experience. You had a lot of sweepstakes superstars here again, but also had a number of new people coming up in the ranks. One of the fun parts of the convention, I guess, is where one of the main speakers asked everyone who had won a car in their lifetime to stand up. He then asked everyone who had won two cars to continue standing up. Then three cars. Then four cars. He kept on doing this until finally one woman was left standing with I believe it was 14 cars won in her lifetime. These winners certainly knew how to win!

But of course, winning sweepstakes would not be possible without the sponsors that host them. So many people were talking about the different companies that sponsored the sweepstakes, and how they felt about them. Many people also thanked the sponsors. We were very fortunate to have a couple sponsors there as well. Both Travalo USA and Kingston technologies were very generous, and donated a number of prizes to be given away. This helped to make the convention fun for everyone. Travalo USA, Sunstar GumBrand, and XShot had been very generous sponsors in the Atlanta convention.

It was a very busy convention, and I think on average I maybe got four hours of sleep a night. Partially it was due to the air-conditioning that blasted on the hour, almost every hour -- apparently a few rooms were being renovated, and mine was one of the lucky ones. However, you could pretty much stop in any hallway in the hotel, and meet people that were sharing stories of their great wins, and tips and strategies of how to continue doing so. I listened and learned a lot. At the same time, I talked a lot too -- so no wonder I drank twice the amount of water I normally would in a week!

But, of course, outside of the convention, we got to do some sightseeing. I joined a few fellow sweepers, and we traveled to a place called Ogden, Utah where we did indoor skydiving. Later, a number of people went on to listen to the famous Mormon Tabernacle choir, who were practicing for an upcoming performance. Finally, I got to do a little bit of sightseeing on my own as well. I got to see the beautiful Park city, which is kind of like the Beverly Hills, California of Utah. The houses there were built on the side of mountains, they were huge, and they were beautiful. The scenery was breathtaking. I also had the opportunity to visit Olympic Park, which is famous for their ski jumps, and past Winter Olympics. There, I also went Zip-Lining -- which, if you've never done that before, essentially sliding down a quarter of a mile of very thin metal cord, about 100 to 150 feet in the air. It was an exhilarating experience.

All in all, I think everyone had a wonderful experience. Many people got to see old friends and catch up over the last year, while other people made new friends. But there was a feeling of camaraderie, enjoyment, and excitement amongst pretty much all of the attendees. And of course, while there – as luck would have it, one woman won $15,000 -- so everyone was excited for her as well!

If you have never been to a sweepstakes convention, but either want to learn more about sweepstakes, make new friends, or simply want to share big winnings of your own that you have had -- then I recommend you attend one. You'll have a chance to make some great new friends, plus have a lot of fun!

Finally – I have to say... the superstars really 'work' at it... Some spend 10+ hours per _day_ entering sweepstakes... So when you have 10,000+ sweepstakes entries in any given month, you are bound to win something!

2014 Orlando Florida Convention

This was a really interesting convention. First off all, the convention was held at a really beautiful, huge, hotel, called the 'Rosen Shingle Creek'. (I am including some photographs of it later on in the book).

It is a hotel resort situated on over 200 acres of land, complete with golf course, swimming pools, outside bars, and much more. Walking from my hotel room to the convention room was actually about one mile long. It took seven to eight minutes just to get there, and I am a tall guy and walk very quickly. I figured that was a sufficient exercise regimen for me – no need to make a special daily trip to the weight/workout room!

I believe there were approximately 750 people in attendance. It was also the 25th Silver Anniversary, so people dressed in more formal attire for the banquet.

One thing that was really funny is as follows. I was doing my best to help as many people as possible, answering questions about sweepstakes/increasing chances of winning, helping them find their way, and so forth. As a result, I ended up missing one of the speaking sessions.

As luck would have it, the speaking session I missed was when I won one of the "grand prizes", an iPad Mini (approximately a $300 value). You needed to be in attendance in order to receive a prize if your name was called. I've wanted an iPad/iPad Mini for a long time, but never purchased one because I figured I would just use it to play computer games. (So I felt that was a smart decision). But if I won one, then that would be okay. Just as the session finished, I met a number of people in the hallway who kept asking me, "Did you hear? You just missed out on a grand prize! You won an iPad mini!" Person after person kept telling me the same thing. I think literally 20 to 30 people let me know. There had been about a hundred prizes given out, and this was one of the last several "big" prizes.

So, of course, I was a bit disappointed. But, I really wanted to win one. So I thought to myself – I am going to make sure I attend the next session, and win it back! I went to the next speaking session fully expecting to win, only surprised to not hear my name called. I thought 'hmm' to myself, and left. I decided to go to the next speaking/prize session anyway. Name after name was called for the smaller prizes, and I had not yet won anything. I was thinking of leaving to quickly go to the restroom, but then they started getting to the grand prizes, there were only several left. So I decided to wait a few minutes. All of the sudden I heard my name called – "Johnathan Wyka-Warzecha – iPad Mini Winner!" I stood up immediately, said 'Yes, I am definitely here!', and accepted my prize.

People laughed and thought it was amazing how I had won the same grand prize a second time. (It was 100% random, as the names were drawn from a ballot drum in front of everyone. So it was very cool how my name got drawn for the exact same prize, a second time!) Some called it poetic justice. I was happy. Since then, I have of course, played a few more hours of computer games on it than I should!

Taste of the MILLIONAIRES! Lifestyle

I decided that this year I wanted to do something amazing and special that people would really love, so had a drawing for a "Taste of the MILLIONAIRES! Lifestyle Sweepstakes". It was sponsored by SweepersChoice. Seven lucky winners would have the chance to feel what it was like to live like a millionaire.

It took me two weeks to prepare. During that time, I was making long distance phone calls to Orlando, making the arrangements, for a truly luxurious experience.

Finally, everything was set.

All seven individuals were instructed to meet in the lobby of the hotel at 6:15 p.m., sharp. No one knew what was going to happen. They just knew that it was something exciting, and were eager with anticipation. They kept trying to get me to spill the secret of what it was. I did not. Then they would ask one another to see if I had tipped anyone off, just a hint of what to expect. No one knew.

Finally, it was time. Everyone got up, and went outside, to be greeted by a super stretch limousine. It was a beautiful, sleek black Chrysler 300, able to seat 12 people. As luck would have it, two of the winners were very experienced as a small camera crew, recording sweeping events, so volunteered to record the entire experience. One by one, the winners entered the limousine, as the driver dressed in a black suit held the door open. Each winner smiled big smiles, excited and unsure of what to expect next.

The limousine drove through Orlando, letting everyone enjoy the beautiful sights. We drove through a richer part of town, called Doctor Philips, and then we finally arrived at our first destination. It was one of the finer, more exclusive upper class restaurants in town, called Eddie V's. The limousine pulled up, and one by one everyone got out, while the camera crew filmed us. Onlookers looked at us, wondering who we were. Were we celebrities, just in town for the night? Part of some new television show? No one knew, but everyone was beaming with smiles.

Finally, we were seated. It was a very posh, expensive, and luxurious restaurant. Many people were dressed in suits. I had arranged to have menus with no prices. Everyone could order from a selection of appetizers, main courses, and finally dessert. I ordered a glass of red wine for everyone, accompanied by sparkling water.

The meal was very delicious, truly lavish dining. Those that ordered steak said it was the best steak they had tasted in their lifetime. I ordered the salmon, basted in garlic creme, it was certainly one of the best I had ever tasted myself.

We were waited on by five different waiters, all with their different functions. One was the main host, another introduced us to the wine, while finally others were responsible for the appetizers and main courses. Our camera crew continued to film the event while others in the restaurant looked on, wondering who we were.

Finally, dessert. Decadent chocolate sundaes, crème brule prepared before our very eyes. The waiter lighted the dessert, and huge blue flames shot up towards the ceiling.

Afterwards, we left. Everyone entered the limousine one by one, while our camera crew filmed. I took photographs of each individual as they entered the limousine, to send to them later.

Excited with anticipation, everyone wanted to know where we were headed next. I smiled, and told them they would know when we got there. Finally, we arrived. I had arranged VIP access to one of the most exclusive night clubs in town that catered to this age group. (Most of the winners were over 40, so this was a 'luxury' night club for that crowd). Everyone had special VIP tickets, which allowed them to go to the front of the line, passing everyone else. Once inside, everyone was ushered to the dance floor, where they could either dance the night away, or enjoy a nice drink while sitting on the cozy leather seats.

Finally, it was time to head home. We did a quick tour of the city, and everyone got to enjoy the beautiful sites in Orlando, Florida. The entire experience was five hours of pure pleasure.

I was very happy that everyone had such an amazing adventure. I wanted them to have a luxurious experience that they would remember for a long time.

Other Activities

I got to have a little bit of fun myself. On the first day, I drove a brand new mustang convertible, the tradition "SweepersChoice" convention car. I invited one of the sweepers to join me, and we had an amazing time touring the city.

Next, I drove a black Mercedes convertible. I knew people really liked Mercedes, and this one was definitely very sleek looking. It had all the bells and whistles, including a seat belt that would automatically tighten itself when you put it on. I drove two of the women sweepers to the airport. It was amazing, they were sisters – but didn't look like sisters. One woman was named Kitty, exceptionally tall (I am not used to looking eye to eye with many people, as I am very tall myself). I learned a lot from both of them, the career paths both had chosen, and their experiences. One worked in Las Vegas, while the other I believe had a video production company. All of us had a wonderful conversation, while enjoying the warm breeze and open air in the convertible.

Finally, I got to drive a beautiful, brand new, yellow 2014 Z06 Corvette. It was a $100,000 car, but looked like a $400,000 Lamborghini. It was fantastic! I got to tour Miami beach with one of the attendees, and even drove down Ocean Drive, a place where many T.V. shows and movies have been filmed!

While in Orlando, I also got to see other amazing sites, such as the Ripley's Believe or Not! museum, as well as WonderWorks. Both had hundreds of interactive exhibits, from historical artifacts, to special effects exhibits that played with your senses. These were located on the touristy 'International Drive' road.

Next, I got to go to a place called 'Gatorland'. I did not realize just how many alligators and crocodiles there are in Florida! A number of us went Zip-lining over the entire park, and got to see an amazing bird's eye view of the gators. Ironically, even though I was 10 minutes away from Disneyland, I never got a chance to go. I guess that is for a future adventure!

Overall it was a truly amazing experience!

Upcoming 2015 Boston Massachusetts Convention

Preparations are already underway for the next national sweepstakes convention. It will be held in Boston Massachusetts at the Sheraton Boston Hotel. If you haven't already, make sure you subscribe to the SweepersChoice newsletter –available at http://www.sweeperschoice.com/ - where we will provide more details as they become available.

For the time being, the information we have is that the convention will be held from September 2nd, 2015 to the September 6th, 2015.

You may find out more details, and sign up here, if you wish to attend: http://www.sweepingboston2015.com/

Winners Circle!

"I have been entering sweepstakes about 30 years. First substantial win was a reel to reel tape player (a dinosaur) now. My husband stopped by a 7-11, got a juice in 1999, and won a trip to Australia. We have won 3 trips to Hawaii -- each one provided different things. For a few years I had enough small prizes to have a drawing for my cafeteria crew at Christmas time. You should have seen this grill cook so excited over a stuffed Taco Bell dog. It has been fun" - Elaine F

SweepersChoice Background

For SweepersChoice, I do have to give some credit to my mother. I happen to be in the computer business. Specifically, software development. My mother loves entering sweepstakes. And she has been doing that pretty much all her life. I remember when I was a kid, it was a big thing around our house when she won a $500 dishwasher. In some ways, we felt like we won the lottery. Not only because it was worth $500, but because now as kids -- we wouldn't have to wash the dishes by hand anymore! (Or so we thought!) Water was still quite expensive, and the dishwasher used a lot of water. So it was really only used for special occasions. We still had to wash the dishes by hand. Oh well.

Fast forward a number of years. One day my mom gives me a phone call. She says, "Hey Johnathan, you're a smart guy...". I kind of thought to myself, "Okay...?" I was wondering where this conversation was going... She then told me how great she thought it would be if there was one place where people could get access to sweepstakes easily. She told me how sometimes it was very time consuming to find and enter sweepstakes, and how a software program would make it so much easier. She told me how she thought a lot of people would benefit from such an application.

I originally resisted, because I felt it would be a "huge" undertaking. And for me, "huge" meant 3-4 weeks. Little did I know at that time, that it would take almost 2 ½ years to develop that software into a workable solution. But, my mother persisted, and so the software was developed. Over the last five years, I don't think there's been one day where I haven't thought about sweepstakes, or talked about it with my mother. (Ironically, she now tells me sometimes I tell her too much about sweepstakes). But hey Mom! You wanted the software, right? :)

Anyways, over the years, I've literally talked to thousands of different people from different walks of life. I've talked to power sweepers -- those people that literally make a living from entering sweepstakes. I've talked to owners of small mom-and-pop shops, to people within large Fortune 500 companies, to find out how they benefit from sweepstakes. And I've talked to friends and family, usually on an almost daily basis, discussing how to make this the best service possible.

And so it's because of all these different experiences, and because of these great people that I talked with, that I'm able to put together these experiences in one book and share with you. I hope you benefit greatly! So without further adieu, let's get started!

Winner's Circle!

"I have been a sweeper for 45 years and have had many great wins... Trips, cash, appliances, a lot of T shirts, caps, watches, snow board, basketball hoop, Disney party for my granddaughter, cosmetics and so much more. It is a hobby that I love. I subscribe to 2 newsletters, do most online and belong to a sweeps club in my area called "A Real Bunch of Winners". This group meets every 2 months and gives me the spur needed to continue. I have had great luck with texting, especially locally. I found out that the local ones are the least entered, especially in the supermarkets." - Patti S.

Winners Circle!

"I have been power-sweeping for the better part of five years. I have won nearly everything you can imagine: cash, trips, electronics, guitars, web-sites, you name it... When I entered sweepstakes to get things I couldn't afford, but could live without it was exciting. There is nothing like a win or receiving a mystery package ... Sweepstaking is hard work and is so much more than just entering. I have many many many stories..." – Shad R.

2. Introduction to Sweepstakes

At first, I was going to dive right in, and start discussing various strategies on how to increase your chances of winning sweepstakes. But then it occurred to me, not everybody is an expert in this area, and might not realize all the benefits. So if you are an expert, feel free to skip to the next section. If you're a little bit new to this, please read on.

What Are Sweepstakes?

Sweepstakes are promotions run by companies, designed to promote their products or services. In exchange for this, people have the chance to win prizes.

The idea is, that people will become engaged with the company brand, and eventually either purchase products or services from the company, or influence other people to do so. They want regular people to know why their product or service is great, and hopefully their long-term sales will outweigh any costs associated with running the promotion.

Many times, companies also have a decision to make. Let's say you have $10,000 designated for marketing. They can either spend that $10,000 making TV commercials, radio commercials, placing newspaper ads, and so forth. Or -- they can take that $10,000, give away a bunch of prizes, and hope that the word-of-mouth advertising is much more effective than the paid advertising.

The really cool thing is that YOU have the power to influence how they spend that money. Do they spend it on advertising? Or do you tell all your friends about the promotion, so that they can offer you chances at winning amazing prizes? The power is in your hands!

Benefits to Entering Sweepstakes

- They are free to enter
- They save you money
- They give you chances to win AMAZING prizes
  (The BIG '4-C's – Cars, Cash, Computers, and Cruises!)
- Usually there are tens of thousands of sweepstakes available in any given month of the year
- You get to make new friends
- It is fun, and exciting

Brief History of Sweepstakes

I was surprised to find that there did not seem to be too much (accurate information) on the 'history' of the sweepstakes available online... I finally did find an out-of-print book... but, it was missing pages, and incomplete... So following is a synopsis of what I did discover, online and from this out-of-print book...

Sweepstakes have been around for a very long time. Like, a VERY long time.

Its origins can be traced back to thousands of years ago, when cultures used 'lots' (random draws) to divide property. Romans cast lots to make arbitrary decisions. Medieval Italians then used prize drawings as sales promotions. As things progressed, American settlers used sweepstakes (and 'lotteries') as fundraising activities for the 'New World'.

However, it's only been in the last 100 years that sweepstakes have really evolved, and become what they are known today. As civilization evolved, new businesses were created – so did the rules surrounding sweepstakes. Sweepstakes evolved so that they could and would be run 'fairly'. Certain criteria were used in determining whether it was a 'true' sweepstakes, such as: (a) What was the idea for the promotion, (b) How was it actually run (to determine fairness), (c) and how could you ensure it was 'legitimate'. Things such as 'no purchase necessary' came into effect. Other countries such as Canada implemented 'skill-testing' questions before a prize could be accepted. (Incidentally – a 'contest' in Canada, means almost <u>exactly</u> the same as 'sweepstakes' in the USA, the main difference being the skill testing question.).

In the 70s and 80s, many people would participate by mailing in entry forms. Other types of promotions required something called a SASE (Self Addressed, Stamped Envelope) to participate in a sweepstakes. The reason for the SASE was to get a 'free' game piece, which you could then use to participate in the sweepstakes. (McDonald's is well known for their Monopoly sweepstakes and game pieces). Many cereal companies ran various promotions that you could participate in. It's only been during the last 10 years or so that there have been things such as 'Online Sweepstakes', and in the last couple years – 'text messaging' sweepstakes.

One thing is certain though, sweepstakes promotions are great ways to raise awareness of a company's products or services. They give regular people the thrill and excitement of being able to win amazing prizes. And the companies benefit from word of mouth advertising.

Types of Sweepstakes, and How to Enter Them

This section will give you a brief overview of the different 'types' of sweepstakes, and how you can increase your chances of winning with them.

Mail-In Sweepstakes (SASE)

This is the 'old-school' way of entering sweepstakes. To enter, you would usually send a SASE (self addressed, stamped envelope) postcard or envelope containing entry information to get a game-piece to participate. (Others, you could just simply send in your entry details through a 3x5 postcard with your name, date of birth, and address information, no SASE required).

Winner's Circle!

"...I think to date my biggest win was a trip to Nashville to a football game and a stay at the Gaylord hotel for 3 nights..." - *Cassandra*

Mail-ins are sweepstakes where you actually have to mail them a letter, in order to get a contest piece or an entry. In the 1990's as well as the early 2000's, you had a very good chance of winning these types of sweepstakes. That was simply because very few people entered. However, because most sweepstakes are now online, available through phones, and so forth -- it's very hard to find these types of sweepstakes.

However, that being said, you can still win them. How? Quite simply, because there are still a lot of large sweepstakes run by companies that require either a UPC symbol, or proof of purchase to enter. And since they **must** offer a free method of entry (otherwise it could be considered a lottery – which in many places would be illegal without a license) -- to obtain a free method of entry, you can request via mail for a game piece/product code in order to participate. Many people do not take the time to do this, giving you very good odds of winning a prize.

You can find mail-ins on your own, or you can subscribe to newsletters that find them for you. While I have not personally used the following service, I do know a number of people that recommend a newsletter called SweepSheet (http://www.sweepsheet.com/). As of this writing, it costs about $100 a year for membership. If this is a type of sweeping you want to consider, then you might want to check this out.

Instant Win Sweepstakes

Online instant Win sweepstakes have become very popular in recent years. Basically, you have the chance of winning one of a number of prizes if you just happen

"Super Tip!"

Use Google alerts to be notified of new sweepstakes. Or, use the 'news' section of Google to scan for brand-new sweepstakes. Of course, as technology changes over time, the method of finding them might change, but the idea will stay the same. You want to be notified as soon as the sweepstakes are launched. If it is an instant Win sweepstakes, chances are very few people know about it yet, so if you enter right away -- the chances of your winning something is very high.

to enter at the right time. Usually, these kinds of sweepstakes will offer hundreds to thousands of smaller prizes, and one or several grand prizes. They also tend to be daily entry, which means that you can enter them every single day. Even though some of the prizes may be "small", they can keep you going and excited about sweeping, and in reality are not that small at all. Many times "Instant Win" sweepstakes tend to have a value of anywhere from $25 to several hundred dollars worth of merchandise.

And of course, you can win them 'instantly'. You will know within minutes if you won or not. So many people like these.

Instant Win sweepstakes are great for companies – because they engage consumers with the brand. And they are great for consumers – because they can get 'instant' gratification – and know if they won right away, or 'instantly'.

Facebook Sweepstakes

Facebook sweepstakes typically require you to "like" their page before you can enter.

As an aside, while at one point in time getting "likes" was very valuable to a company, unfortunately it doesn't really seem to have too much value today. (Before, if someone "liked" a page - it would show up in friends' newsfeeds, and the company would get a lot of word-of-mouth/aka "free" social media advertising. However, because so many companies started doing that, and a few particular game companies really abused it -- Facebook clamped down on that. This really reduced its effectiveness. Chances are you've played one of their games if you've ever used Facebook). So there really is not too much benefit to having a company 'Facebook' page nowadays, unless a company really understands the new way of engaging users. (Most don't). That being said though – there are a LOT of Facebook sweepstakes – and I am assuming you wish to enter them, not host a sweepstakes. :)

So for Facebook sweepstakes, you usually need to do the following.

- Like a Facebook page,
- Allow some kind of 3rd party application to access your personal information
- Enter your personal information/entry details
- Possibly enter a CAPTCHA, play a game, refer friends
- Then FINALLY you get an entry.

Because Facebook sweepstakes tend to be more difficult to enter - and most form fillers do not know how to enter them -- your chances of winning many of them are quite good. You just need to put in the time.

One thing that I've noticed in some forums is that some people are 'afraid' of the 'personal' information that might be shared. While technically speaking, according to Facebooks "Terms of Service" (TOS), you are only 'allowed' to have one Facebook account, many have an account dedicated solely to sweeping.

If you don't have a dedicated account just for sweeping, your privacy concerns may be valid. Depending on what information is passed on, companies 'could' glean extra information such as what college you went to, who your friends are, and what your personal interests are. But, if it is a dedicated account – then they only get what you give them, which would be standard information such as your name, birthdate, and address.

With Facebook sweepstakes, you should be aware that there are hundreds to thousands of people who do nothing but enter Facebook sweepstakes every day. So you should be prepared to wait at least a couple months before you see any winnings from them. It could happen sooner, or it could not. It is just good to know.

Twitter Sweepstakes

A number of companies are offering sweepstakes exclusively through Twitter. Twitter is essentially a platform where individuals can communicate with many people in 140 characters or less. Some individuals have thousands of followers - which simply means that other people like to know what they are thinking.

(As an aside, one video I found hilarious related to how many people use Twitter is called the 'SuperNews – Trouble with Twitter video'. Do a Google search for it, and you should get a number of entries popping up. It looks something like this). It's a very funny video that I think is true for many Twitter users.)

Some companies recognize that these individuals do have influence over what other people think -- so they offer sweepstakes through Twitter with the hopes that they can get recognition for their product or service.

Many times it is simply a matter of "retweeting" the sweepstakes, and the company will pick a random winner. (This simply means that you tell all of your "followers" of the sweepstakes). Other times companies will pick winners based on simply who is following them.

Getting started is rather simple. Simply:

1. Go to Twitter. (http://www.twitter.com/)
2. Create an account. Possibly verify your account by clicking on a link in your e-mail.
3. Use the search functionality in the top right-hand corner of the Twitter website, and search for sweepstakes related terms.

(I.e., "Sweepstakes ", "Win prizes ", etc).

Then, start entering.

Following is a simple glossary of terms.

Follower	Someone who cares about what you think. It simply means that if you write a comment, they will get to see it in their newsfeeds.
Following	It's the people that you want to listen to, in other words the people that you care about what they have to say.
Hashtag	A way of grouping together tweets of a common theme . For example, "#sweepstakes " might be used to find all posts related to sweepstakes.
Tweet	A message that is 140 characters or less to your followers, or someone you are following.

People to 'follow' within the
Sweepstakes Industry

Here are a few individuals or
companies that have a fairly good
reputation within the sweepstakes
industry. You can find out about new
sweepstakes simply by reading what
they post.

https://twitter.com/sweetiessweeps
(Sweeties Sweeps/USA)
https://twitter.com/sweepslovers
(More advertising related type of
sweepstakes site)
https://twitter.com/ContestQueen
(Contest Queen/Canada)

You should note, that in some cases
individuals are paid to promote
specific sweepstakes. Of course, you
can still win from them, but they are
just being paid to promote them.

Winner's Circle!

*"The first time I won
something, it was
1975, and I won $25 at
Walgreens. I was in
college and was down
to my last 50 cents. I
dropped my name in a
fishbowl and it was
drawn. I was able to
buy some groceries for
the rest of the
week...and it was like
manna from heaven. I
have had several wins
over the years but that
one was particularly
memorable because I
was so broke." – Cindy*

You can, of course, find hundreds more people worth following simply by using the search functionality within Twitter.

"Twitter Parties"

I was recently reading about this, and thought it was rather interesting. There are a group of individuals posting something known as Twitter parties. I liken it to hosting a Tupperware party. The gist of it is, you follow a host (the person hosting the party), you talk about a sponsor, and you have a chance to win one of several prizes. For more details, I recommend this link as a good starting point:

http://www.resourcefulmommy.com/category/twitter-parties/

Pinterest Sweepstakes

Because Pinterest is such a relatively new "social network", and because you have to create a new account, and because you have to figure out how it works -- winning these types of sweepstakes are generally pretty easy. Pinterest is basically a place where people 'pin' photographs of things they like, or pictures they like.

Of course, as time goes on, and more people enter these Pinterest sweepstakes, the odds will change. But, I believe at least for the next couple years your chances of winning these -- if you can figure out their system -- will be quite good.

Generally speaking, a company will ask you to "pin" a picture of you using their product or service. Because it requires effort, and because you have to figure out how to do and something in the first place – there are not too many people that do that.

If you want to get started with Pinterest, I recommend doing a Google search to find a tutorial that can walk you through it, step by step.

Video Sweepstakes

Video sweepstakes, generally speaking, have very good chances of winning as well. One sweepstakes/contest I participated in (for Doritos) had a $250,000 prize being offered. At the end of the contest, there were only about 700 entrants. How is that for odds? A 1 in 700 chance at winning $250,000? You can't even find a lottery ticket with odds like that! Amazing! I personally did spend a lot of time on the video, I think about 10 hours, but you don't have to. There were people who probably only spent half an hour to an hour, and still had some very professional looking videos. (I simply wanted to make a cartoon style video). On top of that, I was recently browsing some contest / sweepstakes -- and came across yet another video contest where they were 18 prizes, but only 22 entrants! That meant, pretty much anyone who made a video, was almost guaranteed to win a prize!

That being said, videos, especially nowadays, are not that hard to create, especially if you want to include special effects.

Winner's Circle!

"I thought I'd send you a story on my first and biggest win ever. I entered a contest in Sunset Magazine. It was about how ugly your back yard was. I described mine and I won the contest! I was going through my email when I came across a letter from the magazine saying I won. While I was being skeptical and wondering if it was true, my phone rang. It was a lady from the magazine telling me I had won the contest. I was pretty speechless and to this day I have no idea what at all she said. I caught something about a patio set. So I thanked her and after I had hung up I went back to the email and found out I won a Sunsetter patio set, including a 9 ft umbrella along with a 3 Burner stainless steel gas Bar-B-Q grill and all of it was valued at $2800. I ran to tell my husband and he just smiled and said "Silly, it's a scam". I argued with him that it wasn't because they had not asked for any money, bank accounts or credit cards. I said I really won it. He just smiled. I signed an income tax paper and had to fax it back to the magazine. Still my husband laughed and said you've been scammed. A month went by with no word on when my prizes would be shipped so I emailed the lady and ask when it would be delivered. I was told they were trying to figure out a "prizing" date. By now I was starting to be skeptical too. Another month went by and every time I told someone what I'd won my husband would say, "You didn't win anything and you're not going to get it, someone had a good joke at your expense!" My husband passed away last July believing I had been had. One week to the day after he died the prizes arrived. Sure wish he could have fixed us a couple steaks on the grill and we could have sat under the umbrella at the patio table and had a meal! I could have looked him in the eye and said "I love you, now apologize!" I smile when I sit at the table and think of my husband! Oh and yesterday I got an email from Ryobi tools and I won $500 worth of Ryobi tools of my choice!" – Narda

I will go into more detail of how to enter and win video sweepstakes, later on in this book. Or, you can go to that section now, entitled "How to Win Video Sweepstakes".

Voting Sweepstakes

Voting sweepstakes are almost entirely a different kettle of fish. Unless you're prepared for some extreme competition, I might recommend staying away from these types of sweepstakes. I understand why a company might want to use a voting sweepstakes -- because they believe it will help a lot of people learn about their products or services as other people recruit friends to vote for them, but that's not quite how it happens.

Basically, a voting sweepstakes is as follows. You submit some kind of creative item, as a method of entry into the sweepstakes. It might be taking a photograph, it might be creating a video, it might be writing a short essay. However, a huge difference is that you get a prize based on how many people vote on your entry. In theory, while this sounds like a really nice idea, and that the top quality entries will be chosen by peers -- it's not normally what happens.

Usually what happens is that there a few individuals that are part of vote exchanges. This simply means they are part of a group that exchanges votes. You vote for my entry, and I vote for yours. The problem with this is, that invariably two or three people will get hundreds of votes for their entries, while the rest of the entrants get only a handful. And those two or three entries are not really the best submissions at all. Secondly, if it is a prize with any kind of real value -- doesn't matter what it is -- invariably the second or third place person in the running will accuse the first person of cheating. And they contact the company and say this. The company, being brand-new at a voting sweepstakes -- does not realize that this happens with pretty much every single voting sweepstakes. They may then go ahead and select the second or third place person as the winner, and then there are hard feelings all around.

So unless entries are chosen by a panel of judges, appointed by the company running the sweepstakes -- then I would probably stay away from these voting sweepstakes. You only really have a good chance of winning these if you have a loyal following of several hundred people who will vote for you. And if you do win one of these, then you will need to be prepared to weather the storm when and if runner up accuses you of cheating. It's sad, but true – some people do that, and it's unfortunately just what happens sometimes.

This is one of the very few types of sweepstakes /"contests" that I would recommend staying away from, unless you read the following.

When You Should Participate in Voting Sweepstakes:

The only time I'd recommend you participate in voting sweepstakes is if you meet one or all of the following criteria:

1. **Entries judged by a panel.** If you have a video/photograph/essay/etc that is judged by a 'panel'

of judges that the 'sponsor' appoints, then you have a good chance of winning. I would say these types of sweepstakes are 'impartial' – and entries tend to be closer to what sponsors are looking for. Entries judged by peers (other people entering) are subject to nasty comments, voting groups, etc., etc. that can skew the results.

2. **You have a large following, or access to one.** If, instead, a winner is selected based on the number of peer 'votes' – then you need to make sure you have a large following, or can get someone from a large website/group/forum/newsletter/etc. to support you. The reason is simply because there are organized groups of individuals who have large 'supporters' who will vote for them. You will not be able to win unless you have a large group to vote for you as well.

3. **You have 'last minute' vote supports to prevent 'vote sniping'.** Some people will wait until the very few last minutes of a voting competition to get their 'supporters' to vote for them. That means – say you had 100 entries, and then 2nd place runner had 80 entries. They might wait until the last 20 minutes of the entry period to get all of their "extra" 100 friends to vote. So in the last 20 minutes, they could get 180 entries. By the time you realize what has happened, you are left in the dust with 2nd place, and the competition is closed.

Incidentally, I had something like this happen in real-life when I was in highschool. Whoever could sell the most raffle tickets for a fundraiser would win a CD-player. I was in the lead with about 100 tickets of about 100 students. The 2nd place entrant I believe only had 30-40 tickets sold. About 1 hour before the competition 'officially' ended – (I think it had been running for a week) -- he went around to all his friends, asking them to give him their ticket stubs (since they had no chance of winning with only 5-10 tickets sold each). He then shows up with something like 105 ticket stubs, and won the CD player. I was shocked and dismayed. However, after the prize was awarded, the teacher quickly found out what happened from other students, and that the winner had 'cheated'. Unfortunately though, he had already given away the prize. To the teacher's credit though – he did take me aside and ask me if there was anything he could do to make it up. Being a young student, I never thought of asking him to get another CD player (I didn't think it would be 'right'), so just said no and walked away. But – you can bet that if this can happen in highschool, then it can surely happen in the 'real' world where the stakes are much higher.

"Mommy" Blogs/RaffleCopter

There are something called Blog sweepstakes. Generally speaking, they tend to be stay-at-home moms that review various products for sponsors. The average value of such prize tends to be about $25.

Recently, in the last couple years, something called "Rafflecopter" has become very popular for these types of sweepstakes. All a blogger does is customize the look and feel of the sweepstakes entry page, and then insert the entry page into their blog posts. One thing that has helped make Rafflecopter so popular amongst these blogs, is that as a condition of entry, you need to "like" one or more Facebook pages. Unfortunately though, most of these blogs go a little crazy, become spammy, and have 50 or more pages that you need to like for "bonus" entries. So it is not uncommon to see something like "150,000 entries" into the sweepstakes, when in reality it might only be 200 or so people with 1000 entries each.

Many times, finding a "legitimate" Mommy blog prize giveaway can be hard. I have heard many stories of individuals that had hundreds or thousands of entries, only to see a prize given away to someone with one entry. And then it turns out that person with one entry was a friend or family member of the blog owner. So how do you determine whether it is legitimate or not? Simply look at who has won the last 10 or 15 prizes. If you see a similar group of people all winning all the time, then chances are these prizes are just being given away to friends and family, and you can avoid them in the future.

Furthermore, there is a group of about 100 or so women that cross promote these types of Rafflecopter sweepstakes. They have a private forum where they share tips and strategies. If you start your own blog, you can probably find out how to join this group simply by contacting one of the women running a Rafflecopter sweepstakes, and/or 'Mommy' blog.

"Regular" Blog Sweepstakes

Regular blog sweepstakes tend to be a little bit more legitimate. They tend to be run by companies, as opposed to individuals (or at least individuals with more of a 'company' style focus), and simply use the blog as a way of connecting with their customer base. Some such blogs include Steamy Kitchen, Rasa Malaysia and Need Coffee. They have their own content, but then add regular sweepstakes to "spice up" a user's reading experience. These types of blogs tend to have a good chance of your winning a prize.

Text Message/MOBILE Sweepstakes

Text message or mobile sweepstakes are starting to become more and more popular. Generally speaking, to enter, you send a text message to what is known as a "short number". Once you send a text message, a company has your contact information and can contact you if you win.

Sometimes, however, people are concerned that if they enter too many text message sweepstakes, they will be inundated with text messages. And then, their cell phone might become useless because they receive so many marketing messages. This is a valid concern.

Fortunately, however, there are alternatives. You can still participate in these text message sweepstakes, and not worry about it affecting your regular phone. I do, of course, recommend periodically reading the newsletters that the company sends out, because after all that is one way of supporting them when they run sweepstakes. However, you can then use your phone for personal messages -- and your special text message account for sweepstakes.

Sending Text Messages without a Phone

There are several different ways of doing this. Wireless

Secret TIP/Strategy

As an aside, while not 'technically' a sweepstakes (actually, it isn't), I know of a landlord for an apartment building who has a fairly profitable side business related to going through recycling bins.

In his building, there are big recycling bins at the bottom of the building. Once a week, he goes through it and looks for any pop/soda cans, crushes them, an then takes them into a store to get money for recycling. He gets about $300 a week for spending may be 3 to 4 hours doing this. So, it's a nice extra $1200 a month, simply because he brings the crushed cans into the store, to be recycled.

So, if you are in an apartment building looking for PIN codes, and also notice that no one else i recycling the bottles, you might find it brings a little bit of extra income for yourself as well.

carriers have an e-mail address especially reserved for only text messages. If you know what this text message e-mail is, then you can send text messages to them to your heart's content. However, that can be a very time-consuming process, and there are easier alternatives.

Basically, what you would do is, find free or paid service on the Internet that sends text messages. As of this writing, several such services include http://www.txt2day.com/, and http://www.smseverywhere.com/ . If you want a paid service that might have additional features to make it easier for you to manage text messages, then you can use something like http://www.TXTSignal.com/.

Using services such as the above can help you participate in text message sweepstakes without worrying about getting an excessive amount of 'text-message' spam. At the same time though, make sure you support the sponsors by telling your friends or family of sweepstakes, and/or periodically reading the newsletters and text messages that they send to your account.

PIN Codes/UPC Symbols

While all sweepstakes must have a free method of entry, sometimes it is not really practical to obtain that free method of entry. For example, there **are** a number of sweepstakes which will give you a free entry, such as a PIN code, but you have to send a SASE envelope. (So in some respects, you could say it costs you $.50 for postage and envelope to get an entry, plus your time). So if you wanted to say, get 50 PIN codes to get 50 entries, that would cost you $25 for postage and envelopes.

So, what some people do as an alternative is to go through people's recycling and look for pop bottle/soda PIN codes, beer PIN codes, or UPC symbols from various products. While I would personally never do this (it's just not my 'thing') – I do know of people who do and are very successful with it.

Many people many people simply throw out the bottles with the PIN codes, and never even bother looking to see if they won anything. The thing is, though, many times there are winning codes that are thrown out.

There was a story in 2006 that made headlines when a girl accidentally threw away a cup with a PIN code, and another girl found the cup, with a winning PIN for a $32,000 SUV vehicle. Taken directly from Wikipedia: (source: http://en.wikipedia.org/wiki/ Tim_Hortons)

"In March 2006, two families were fighting over the Toyota RAV4 SUV prize of C$32,000 value when their daughters found a winning "roll up the rim" coffee cup in a garbage bin of an elementary school in Saint-Jérôme, north of Montreal. The younger girl had found a cup in the garbage bin and could not roll up the rim, so requested the help of an older girl. Once the winning cup was revealed, the older girl's family stated that they deserved the prize. Tim Hortons originally stated that they would not intervene in the dispute. A further complication arose

when Quebec lawyer Claude Archambault requested a DNA test be done on the cup. He claimed that his unnamed client had thrown out the cup and was the rightful recipient of the prize. On 19 April 2006, Tim Hortons announced that they had decided to award the prize to the younger girl who had initially found the cup."

So, you never know what you could find. Plus, there is a major side benefit. Many of the companies that offer prizes through PIN codes also tend to have membership sites where they will let you redeem gifts & prizes for collecting a certain number of "points". One of the more well-known ones happens to be Coca-Cola. (Details here: http://www.mycokerewards.com/).

I know of many people who have gotten free food and free merchandise simply by collecting points. I also read about a lady who got about $20,000 worth of merchandise in a year simply by collecting break open tickets (promotional theme pieces) that people threw away as they were leaving Safeway stores.

Of course, this is not the most sanitary way winning free prizes. So, if you're going to start going through someone else's recycling bins, I recommend wearing gloves and of course keep yourself clean. Quite simply, because it could get a little messy if you spilled some soda on yourself, or other food.

Instagram/VINE

Instagram and VINE are two 'relatively' new methods of entering online sweepstakes. Both are designed to be used with iPhones, iPads and Android devices. Because they are so new, your chances of winning prizes, if you enter, are very high. (As a matter of fact, Heinz 57 had a promotion for $25,000. Before I promoted it to my list – there were only about 50 photographs, or roughly 10 entrants. After my promotion, there were 350. But still, that was very low for a chance to win $25,000! I will get into more detail about that shortly...)

Instagram is basically a service designed to allow you to share photographs and videos with others, through cellphones. With Instagram, you can also take videos. Because it has been brought to Facebook, it is getting a lot more exposure. Until recently, you could not view any photos unless you had a phone with the app installed. Fortunately though, you now can through this website: http://web.stagram.com/

As of this writing, I found an excellent guide that gives an overview of Instagram here. The writer is based in the UK, so refers to sweepstakes as "comps" or "competitions":

http://www.compersnews.com/comping-guides/
CompingGuide_Instagram.pdf

Vine is a competing product from Twitter, designed to allow you to take six second videos. According to their website, they are basically 'video' tweets. (Short messages, but in 'video' format).

Some companies and promoters are experimenting with both formats to see how successful they are. Although "young" people tend to be the ones using these types of technologies, they don't tend to actually 'enter' sweepstakes because they find it too 'time-consuming'.

This is good news for you though. Very few people know how to 'enter' these types of sweepstakes. So, if you take about 15-20 minutes to invest in learning how to use these two technologies, when you see these types of sweepstakes you will have very good odds of winning.

Flash Sweepstakes

You don't see many of these types of sweepstakes around, but they still exist. Flash sweepstakes simply refer to sweepstakes that use Flash technology. (The technology from Adobe lets you watch videos, play computer games, and much more).

I thought it was worth mentioning these types of sweepstakes, simply because most form fillers cannot fill them in. (SweepersChoice actually can, however it is not publicly available at the moment). So – since most form fillers cannot fill them in – people look at entering them as 'work'. And this is good news for you – because it means your chances of winning a prize if you enter are very high!

So when you see a 'Flash' type sweepstakes, make sure you enter!

Alternative Methods of Getting Free Stuff

While the following methods are technically not sweepstakes or contest, you can usually get cash, or points that can be redeemed for merchandise by doing the following:

- **Entering online surveys.** While there is a lot of garbage out there, some surveys are legitimate and can pay you $.50 to a few dollars for each completed survey. I recommend asking around first to find the legitimate ones.

- **Tweeting and blogging for cash.** If you have any kind of following on Twitter, YouTube, or your Facebook account, some companies will pay you $5-$10 just to connect with your audience. (Of course, read the terms and services of the social network you're using to make sure it is okay for what you're promoting.)

  In fact – do a Google search for things like "Sponsored Posts", "Sponsored Tweets", "Sponsored Facebook Posts", and so forth. There are actually 'marketplaces' where you can "rent" your following for $5-$10 at a time. (If you choose to do this, though, – I recommend only promoting products or services you genuinely believe in. Otherwise your readers/followers/etc will quickly stop listening to what you have to say. One of them happens to be "Sponsored Tweets", located here: http://www.sponsoredtweets.com/)

The Future

The future is constantly changing, and there are will be brand-new social networks that exist today that you can't even think of now. Obviously, you're going to see more and more mobile sweepstakes in the near future. You are also going to see brand-new social networks popping up that do not exist today. You can significantly increase your chances of winning these types of sweepstakes, simply by entering when you find out about them. This will be <u>simply because not a lot of people know about them.</u>

As of this writing, Pinterest is the new kid on the block. Even though I am personally very involved in the sweepstakes industry -- that is to say, making it easy for people to enter them – even I am not that familiar with Pinterest, yet. However, I have started seeing more and more new sweepstakes encouraging users to link to their Pinterest board in order to get an entry to a sweepstakes.

Another interesting note, recently Heinz 57 (the ketchup company) was running a $25,000 sweepstakes, over the course of one month. All a user had to do was take a creative picture of themselves showcasing Heinz, and they had their chance to win a share of $25,000. The caveat was they had to post the picture to Instagram. Three weeks into the promotion (with only one week left), they had only about 50 entries. (And in reality, it looked like the existing contestants had submitted multiple pictures. This meant that quite possibly the "actual" number of individuals participating was about 10 people. This means, if you submitted a picture, you had a 1 in 10 chance of winning their share of $25,000). I sent out an e-mail to my list of 10,000+ users, and a week later there were 350 entries. Imagine having a 1 in 350 chance of winning $25,000! This is an example of how new technology that is difficult for people to adapt to can give you amazing odds at winning prizes! For $25,000, those are exceptional odds. And I am hoping to hear back soon, to hear whether one of my readers won one of the prizes. (Edit: Since the first publication of this book, I actually found out that one did ☺)

Ironically, you're probably also going to find that the "old methods" become more and more successful as well. Such as radio sweepstakes, mail-in sweepstakes, and so forth. Simply because most people go with the 'path of least resistance', and this includes entering sweepstakes. If you have to 'phone' in to a radio station, for some people that is 'work'. But for you, that means better odds of winning prizes.

And, as the saying goes, the more things change, the more they stay the same. In 1999, I created an online scratch and win game, written in Java. Companies could purchase the software and create their own custom scratch cards. And, as a matter of fact, even one of the promotional departments at Microsoft purchased a copy of my software to promote a new version of Windows. (So I can actually say that "Microsoft" uses my software!) 10 years later, I ran into a girl running a "brand-new revolutionary business". She even auditioned for the T.V. show "Dragons Den" that features entrepreneurs seeking investment. You know what her idea was? Creating a scratch and win card game application for the iPhone. Functionality and purpose-wise, her idea was pretty much exactly the same as my idea and software program -- I think she was even applying for a patent for it. The only difference was that it was designed to work on an iPhone, instead of the desktop computer.

So bottom line, keep learning. Learn how to enter the newest style of sweepstakes, while entering existing sweepstakes. You'll significantly increase your chances of winning amazing prizes.

3. How to Increase Your Chances of Winning Sweepstakes

This chapter will be fairly comprehensive, in that it will outline a whole bunch of different strategies on how to increase your chances of winning. I recommend reading this entire section, because there are probably many things you have not thought of. Everything from how you interact with the companies holding the sweepstakes, to getting friends and family involved.

But before you can enter to win them, you need to be able to find them. So the first section discusses that, and then discusses a number of additional strategies on how to win certain types of sweepstakes, as well as sweepstakes in general. Finally, this chapter shows you how you can get products for free in exchange for helping to promote products and services from various companies.

Winner's Circle!

"Biggest wins -- Trip to the Grammys & Hotel, Steve Morse Musicman Signature Model Guitar, worth 3,000.00, a Nosler Rifle worth 2500.00"
– Michael P.

How to Find Sweepstakes

It's funny, I almost left out this section of the book. However, it is very important. I am going to be telling you how you can find sweepstakes yourself through search engines, online website forums, and more. Of course, you can use software such as SweepersChoice (http://www.sweeperschoice.com/) to greatly speed up this process. However, that will be discussed later in the tools and resources section of this book.

With respect to the search engines segment, I have to give credit to someone named Steve. He gave an excellent presentation at the 2013 Utah sweepstakes convention discussing online search methods. While I already knew most of the techniques he discussed, I did learn a few things that I will also be sharing here. And it reminded me that I definitely needed to include a segment on that in this book! So, let's get started!

Online Website Forums Prize Finding Strategies

There are a number of websites devoted to discussing nothing except sweepstakes. Some of the more popular ones include FindPrizesNow.com, SweepsAdvantage.com, Online-Sweepstakes.com, and of course SweepersChoice.com. On these websites, you can usually find thousands of sweepstakes for you to enter on a monthly basis. These directories tend to be constantly updated with fresh content.

The FindPrizesNow.com website contains a very comprehensive list of regularly updated sweepstakes across the USA. (http://www.findprizesnow.com/)

You simply click on the type of prize that you want to win,

whether it is a cash prize, an automobile, a vacation, or more. The directory then lists all the sweepstakes that we have found related to that category. You then simply click on that link, visit the company website, and then enter for your chance to win. Here is a sample screenshot of what you might see:

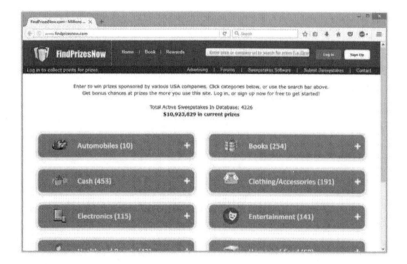

Many other websites contain sweepstakes listings as well. So it is definitely worth visiting a number of different sweepstakes directories.

I list a number of these directories, website forums, and so forth that you can access later on in this book. If you wish to go there now, simply look for the "Website Resources" section of this book, then "Sweepstakes Websites".

While many sweepstakes directories contain thousands of sweepstakes, they are not usually that comprehensive. That is simply because, in any given month, there are probably literally tens of thousands sweepstakes being run across the USA to promote various companies, and so it is difficult for one site to find and list them all. So make sure you find and use several good sources for sweepstakes.

So, that leads me to the next section.

Search Engines - Prize Finding Strategies

One of the biggest things that helps you increase your chances of winning, are the number of entries that you get, relative to how many people enter. Sometimes, companies do not know how to promote their sweepstakes. So, if you can find those sweepstakes and enter them, you have excellent chances of winning. Search engines can be extremely effective tools at finding these "Golden Nugget" sweepstakes.

Some of the more popular search engines to use in order to find sweepstakes are:

- Google

Tip: How to find only Facebook sweepstakes

There are a number of promotional companies that sponsor 'Facebook' sweepstakes. To get a list of current Facebook sweepstakes, you can use the following Google search:

sweepstakes site:www.facebook.com -posts -posted -ogn -topic -search -story_fbid

- Yahoo
- Bing

For this section, I am going to be discussing how to use the Google search engine. However, other search engines such as Yahoo, and Bing operate in a similar fashion. To get more details on the different search engines, simply visit the respective website, and read their usage instructions.

"Search Operators" – Finding EXACTLY what you want

While many people know that they can go to a search engine to find "stuff", many do not know how to refine their search to find exactly what they are looking for. You need to use something called a "search operator" to 'drill down' into your search.

For example, if you simply type in the word sweepstakes, you would get a list of sweepstakes -- but you might also get some from the year 2000, you might get ones from all over the world, or might get ones that you're not interested in. Fortunately, there is a way of specifying exactly what you want.

i) Let's say you wanted to win a computer. Then you could include the phrase "win a computer" in your search. So it would look something like this:

```
sweepstakes "win a computer"
```

However, you might end up finding a bunch of "contests" as well (since Google figures 'contests' are similar to 'sweepstakes). Contests might say require you to write an essay on why you want to any computer. If you only wanted the ballot type of entries, then you might add a search operator to refine your search. You would simply use the minus sign (-) to tell the search engine what you do not want to find, in this example, "contests".

So now all of a sudden, your search query might look like this:

```
sweepstakes "win a computer" -contests
```

But now, while this is good, it is not great. This is because the USA is not the only country that offers sweepstakes. You might find sweepstakes from Australia, Canada and the UK.

So to further refine your search, you might specify the 'country', as well as 'exclude' specific websites. (For example, some Canadian websites end in ".ca", while Australian websites end in ".au").

So, you might refine your search now, to look something like this:

```
sweepstakes "win a computer" -contests -
site:.au -site:.ca
```

This will help you find more of what you're looking for. However, again, we have another situation. Search engines like to index old content is well. So it is possible, that you may be finding sweepstakes from several years ago. So, you can also ask the search engines to find sweepstakes that that have the year 2013 listed in them. So now your search query would look something like this:

```
sweepstakes "win a computer" -contests -
site:.au -site:.ca 2013
```

Again though, let's take this a little bit further. Let's say you've only wanted to find Facebook sweepstakes. Then, you could include the "site" operator to specify the website that you want to search. So now your search query might look something like this :

```
sweepstakes "win a computer" -contests -
site:.au -site:.ca 2013 site:facebook.com
```

But what about giveaways? They are similar to sweepstakes. Well, you can simply add the "or" operator. And, you need parentheses around it.

So for example, now your search for it would look like this

```
(sweepstakes or giveaway) "win a computer"
-contests - site:.au -site:.ca 2013
site:facebook.com
```

One thing that is nice though, is you can *still* fine-tune your search even further. Similar types of sweepstakes, tend to use similar types of wording. For example, you can search for "photo contests" which tend to have fairly good odds. This is because, for a lot of people, uploading a photograph is a lot of work. So if there are only a few entries, you have a very good chance of winning it.

So, let's say we wanted to do the same search we've been doing so far, but now want to find photo contests. You might remove the "-contests" operator, but now add "upload an original image".

So now your query might look like this :

```
(sweepstakes or giveaway) "win a computer"
"upload an original image" - site:.au -
site:.ca 2013 site:facebook.com
```

Sometimes though, contests are judged. This means that you really only have a chance of winning, if it is exactly what the company is looking for, or is of professional quality. Fortunately though, there are contests that do not judge the entries, but simply require photographs, videos, essays, and so forth. Perhaps a sponsor simply wants an assortment of pictures that they can use for promotion, so they don't really care exactly what it looks like. In this case, you might use the following terminology to find exactly what you're looking for:

"not judged" - find easy to enter contests, that are not judged based on quality
"random drawing" - again, looking for something that is a random drawing

So, in the above example, you might use a search query like this:

```
(sweepstakes or giveaway) "win a computer"
"upload an original image" "not judged" -
site:.au -site:.ca 2013 site:facebook.com
```

Finally, there are some judging agencies that indirectly or directly sponsor a lot of sweepstakes. You can search for them directly, by using terms such as "wildfire", "woobox", "eprize", and so forth.

If you have an 'idea' of what you are looking for, you can also use an asterisk (*) to do something called a "wildcard search". This means, that you can match a phrase that starts with something, and fills in the blanks for the rest of the search. For example, you could do a search for sweepstakes that appear in the month of July. It might look something like this:

```
(sweepstakes or giveaway) "win a computer"
"upload an original image" "not judged" -
site:.au -site:.ca "ends July *, 2013"
site:facebook.com
```

The above query would find everything that had text "ends July ____, 2013" in it. This would be really useful for finding sweepstakes that will expire soon.

And one final note, some companies are doing something called "flash" sweepstakes. I don't mean "flash" in terms of Adobe flash. I mean "flash" in terms of sweepstakes that might last one week, one day, or even only a couple hours. You can use a search engine to find these, as well as Google alerts, to increase your chances of winning prizes.

Super Tip!

If you want to have really good chances of winning prizes, you can look for local sweepstakes. Many times, whether a sweepstakes is local will be specified in the rules, and contain phrasing along the lines of "open to residents of New York" or "open to New York residents only". Since the sweepstakes is restricted to a specific geographical location, then the chances of other people entering are low, while your chances of winning are really high!

Now fortunately, there is an easier way of doing some of what I just mentioned. Google has a point-and-click interface, as well as an advanced search form, that might make it easier to do searches.

As of this writing, when you do a Google search, you can click on the search tools button to further refine your search. This could be useful in the following way. You can find "recent" sweepstakes simply by clicking on the past week the second red circle. This means that Google would list all sweepstakes that found in the last week. This could be especially useful for you for "instant win" types of prizes. This is simply because sometimes it takes a company a few days to really get going with their sweepstakes promotion. If you happen to be one of the first people to enter, then you may have exceptional chances of winning some instant win prizes, simply because no one else is entering.

A final note. Search engines are becoming easier and easier to use. Over the last 10 years, personalization and contextual analysis has become a lot better. This simply means that, as you use a search engine, the search engine gets smarter and has a better idea of what you're looking for in the future. As technology changes, so will the methods of finding information. If you keep abreast of the latest developments, you can

significantly increase your chances of winning prizes.

How to Win Video Sweepstakes

I personally have entered a number of video sweepstakes, so have a good understanding of what is necessary to win. That being said, I still learned a few things at the convention and will be sharing what I know and what I learned, with you.

Finding Video Sweepstakes

First of all, you need to know where to find the sweepstakes. Obviously, you can use Google to search for sweepstakes and make sure you include key words like "submit video", "upload a video", "submit a video", and so forth. However, there are also websites that specialize in talking only about video sweepstakes.

You can use websites such as the following:

- OnlineVideoContests.com
- FilmTheNext.com
- VidoPP.com

These are not the only types of video contest websites out there though. Do a little research, and you can find more.

You may also use regular sweepstakes directories, such as FindPrizesNow.com, SweepsAdvantage.com, and Online-Sweepstakes.com to find video sweepstakes.

One interesting point that was mentioned at the convention that I agree with is that sometimes professional film students tend to get involved with the "video contest only" types of websites. Of course, you can still win, but it may be harder, and it is just something to keep in mind. The speaker at the convention mentioned that he was persistent nevertheless, and submitted something like 70 videos for one particular sweepstakes to significantly increase his chances of winning. And, he did.

Necessary Equipment to Enter Video Sweepstakes

To enter video sweepstakes, you don't really need a lot of fancy equipment. However, if you can spend a couple hundred dollars on getting

How one man won 15+ BIG SCREEN 50" HD T.V.s in the course of several months

I was talking with someone at the 2013 Utah convention who had ended up winning something like 15+ 50" HD BIG screen T.V.s in a matter of months. I asked him what his secret was.

He was entering 'regional' sweepstakes in the truest sense of the word.

It turned out that a company was having a promotion, whereby each store location was giving away one prize. It was restricted specifically to that store. But you also had to do something like submit a UPC symbol.

He went from store to store, submitted UPC symbol, after UPC symbol, and entered. Apparently very few people did this. Lucky for him, several months later, he was the proud owner of 15+ big screen T.V.'s! He had his Christmas shopping done!

good quality equipment to produce good quality video, then you can significantly increase your chances of winning. This is simply because if the sponsor can't understand what you are saying, or the video is not that clear, they may just move onto the next submission.

If you have purchased a laptop within the last couple years, or have an iPad, then chances are pretty good you already have some kind of video recording device built into the machine. This is simply called a WebCam. If you look at the programs preinstalled on your computer, then chances are you will find software specifically designed to help you make WebCam videos. You simply push a button, it records the video, and then you're done. However, sometimes the video quality as well as sound quality can be quite poor. This can affect your chances of winning a video sweepstakes, so I recommend purchasing the following equipment.

Good quality camera - You do not need to spend a fortune for a fancy camera. I have gone to stores like Best Buy, and seen excellent, but inexpensive, cameras that would suit my needs. Basically, the main criteria you're looking for in finding a good camera is as follows.

- It needs to be able to record high quality video, generally speaking with at least a 1024x768 resolution. Usually, you are talking about a minimum of 1 megapixel in resolution.

- Ideally, it would have options on the camera to customize the lighting. It is not 100% necessary, but helps you make better quality videos.

- Image stabilization. This simply means that if you are filming while holding the camera, the image does not look shaky.

- Optionally – it will have somewhere that you can plug an external microphone into. This helps increase sound quality.

- And obviously, can record video. Most cameras you purchase nowadays include that by default.

I purchased a new camera about six or seven years ago, for about $350. It still does an excellent job today. You do not have to spend thousands of dollars to get a good quality video.

Good quality microphone - At the very least, I recommend getting a headset. You can buy these in most stores for only about $25-$30. However, if you are looking for something better, you can spend upwards of $100. I personally use something called the "Yeti Microphone", from www.bluemic.com. I believe it cost me about $150, but it has done a fantastic job of producing very good quality audio. Of course, you don't need something that expensive -- unless you really want to produce fantastic audio files. Before that, I was using $30 headsets that suited my needs. I decided to purchase this particular microphone to give me that added quality.

Now that you have the necessary equipment, you can move on...

Preparing a Script for the Video

Unless you are fantastic at "ad-libbing" (which simply means thinking of things to say or do on the spot) - then I recommend preparing some kind of script before you start filming. It was a recommendation someone gave me a long time ago, and I have benefited greatly from it since then.

If you try recording video while thinking of what to say, then you tend to say "um, ah, hmm, ahh" a lot. And instead of people focusing on what you have to say, or watching your videos, they will instead actually start counting the number of times that you say "um". Think about it – haven't you done that before? And if you're trying to win a video contest, that is the last thing that you want to do.

Secret Video Design Strategies

Now, you have the tools to create the video.

Fortunately, there are also some secret 'design' strategies that make your job a lot easier. I am going to cover the most popular and effective ways of creating good quality videos.

iPhone/Phone Videos (Including Special Effects):

These are probably the easiest types of videos to create, and almost everyone knows how to do it. If you don't, you can have a friend, son, daughter or spouse show you how to do that kind of thing within a couple of minutes. The "tricky" part I suppose you could say would be uploading the video to your computer. For that, I recommend doing a Google search and typing in something like the following : "how to copy a video from a phone to a computer" and then you might even include the type of phone you are using. I.e., (iPhone, Samsung galaxy, etc. etc.) There are some very good tutorials online that will show you how to do this step by step.

The cool thing is, is that there are apps that can add special effects to your videos. Some of these only cost one or two dollars for some very professional Hollywood style effects. Simply adding these effects give you quite an edge in terms of winning. One such example is something called Hollywood **"Action Movie FX"**. It adds really cool special effects to your videos, such as Hollywood special effects such as helicopters, explosions, plus much more. If you've never heard of it before, simply go to the iTunes store and do a search for that. You can also do a youtube search for "Action Movie FX" to see some premade videos of the special effects that you can add. The quality of your video is only limited by your creativity. And this can help give you an advantage.

Animoto – Auto Creation of Videos

Making videos does not have to be hard. Another really good, really useful tool is something called Animoto. All you have to do is to upload a bunch of pictures to a video site, and the software automatically creates a very professional looking video. It includes music, transitions, and special effects. You can literally create a video 3 to 4 minutes, and then have something very professional that you can submit as a contest entry. Do this a few times, and not only will you have a very creative video, but you also have some amazing chances at winning some amazing prizes. You can get more details here: http://www.animoto.com/

They do have a free version, as well as several paid versions. I recommend first trying out the free version, and if you like it, upgrade to the paid version, for at least a month, to try it out. (The $25/month version allows you to easily remove branding at the end of the video). If you do go for the $25 version, then make sure you use it. Make at least 10 or 15 videos, submit them to video sweepstakes, and see if you win anything. They also do have a $3/month version - but that will include their logo. And I do not recommend doing that for any sweepstakes you submit to, because the (sweepstakes) company probably would not like seeing a 3rd party logo.

"Cartoon" Style Video Creation in Less than 5 Minutes

Youtube (owned by Google) recently acquired a number of companies that allow you to easily create cartoon style videos. As of this writing, you can get access to those video creation tools by going here: http://www.youtube.com/yt/creators/

My personal favorite was XtraNormal (http://www.xtranormal.com/), as I found it created very high quality cartoon videos. (Sadly, as of July 2013, they discontinued the service). However, you can find very similar style services through YouTube's video creation services, as well as several links that I include below.

Other tools & services include GoAnimate (http://goanimate.com/) , as well as StupeFlix, (http://studio.stupeflix.com/en/) . All worth checking out. Especially if you want to win some major video prizes.

Sony Vegas Studio

This is a fantastic program that you can get relatively

inexpensively. I've probably created hundreds of videos using this software. There is a little bit of a learning curve, but it is worth the investment. It allows you to easily stitch videos clips together, add audio files, as well as apply a number of special effects and special transitions. Sony Vegas has several different versions of the software ranging from $50, all the way up to about $1000. But you really don't need the super expensive version, because the $50 version will do a fantastic job. (The more expensive versions are really only if you were looking to create 'movie' quality video, complete with sound and special effects).They also had add-ons that you can purchase, such as sound loops, video loops, and more -- to give your video that professional quality touch.

But you should probably only get the software if you want to start making professional videos, and have some time to invest in learning how to use it.

Conclusion:

Creating videos does not have to be that hard, and because so few people do it -- you have some amazing chances at winning some great prizes. This is especially true, when you can easily find video sweepstakes that only have a handful of entries, but some really sweet prizes.

How to Win Instant Win Sweepstakes

There are a few things you can do to increase your chances and likelihood of winning an instant Win sweepstakes. Instant Win prizes tend to be evenly distributed over the course of the day, and over the entire course of the promotional period.

So for example, this means that if there were 100 prizes being awarded within one month, then most likely there would be three winners today. Secondly, chances are one prize will be awarded in the morning, one prize in the afternoon, and one prize in the evening.

With this knowledge, you can significantly increase your chances of winning instant Win sweepstakes, and here's how.

1. Enter early in the morning or late at night - Most people settle down or get ready for bed around 9 or 10 P.M. However, sometimes this is a great time to enter an instant win, because everyone else is sleeping and your chances of winning are very good. Likewise, most people don't get up until about 6 or 7 A.M. in the morning, to get ready for work. If you are up earlier than that, and enter when no one else is, then you can also significantly increase your chances of winning a prize.

2. Enter daily. If you can't do daily, do it at the very beginning, or middle to the end of the promotion time period. For most companies running instant win sweepstakes, it is difficult for them to create sustainable interest in the promotion. What this means, is that they will spend a lot of money to initially promote the sweepstakes, and get a lot of interest, but very quickly (and unfortunately) the hype decreases, and people don't enter the sweepstakes.

What this means for you, is that if you enter sweepstakes right at the start – before they begin promoting heavily – then you have a very good chance of winning a prize. Also, you have good chances towards the middle or end of promotion since the company is not spending any more money on promoting the sweepstakes. So many times, they will have a lot of extra, unrewarded prizes. And of course, for you -- this is good! Because if you enter, the likelihood of you winning something is quite good!

3. Join a sweepstaking club, and share the sweepstakes. If only one person is entering the promotion at a time, you may or may not win something. But if you have four or five people all entering at the same time, the chances of one of the winning is greatly increased. You can also have friends and family enter for you as well.

4. Certain times of the day. Sometimes a sweepstakes may be at the 'same' time, every day. (Some sponsors do this). So, if a friend tells you about a daily instant win that they won, ask him/her at what time they won. There is a 'chance' that you may be able to win something as well if you enter at exactly the same time, the next day. Especially if it is a 'daily' instant win game.

5. Enter on Holidays. If it is Christmas, Easter, Mother's Day, or a holiday like Independence Day – then enter! Many people take 'breaks' on these days – which means it is very likely that there are very few people entering. If you happen to enter on a holiday, then you can significantly increase your chances of winning an instant win prize!

How to Win "Mail-In" sweepstakes

While 'mail-in' sweepstakes are getting fewer and far between, from time to time there are still 'mail-in' only types of sweepstakes. Over the years, these are strategies sweepers have used to increase the likelihood of winning:

- **Use colored envelopes.** The rationale is that when a sponsor receives it, it 'stands out' more.

- **Use envelopes with images on them.** Similar rationale as point #1.

- **Write Clearly.** You would be surprised how many people have 'poor' handwriting. Make sure you print your name and address *clearly,* such that a sponsor can actually *read* it should you be chosen as a winner. We actually had run a promotion where we had to 'pass' on a potential winner, – simply because we couldn't read what he or she wrote, and didn't know where to send a prize!

How to Increase Your Chances of Winning In-Store Sweepstakes!

This section is also from the SweepersChoice Strategy Guide. You may move on if you've read this before. Otherwise, it's great information! It will show you how you can increase your chances of winning 'local' sweepstakes.

1. Pay attention to ballot boxes wherever you are!

Whether you are shopping, banking, buying some cookies at a local bakery, etc, pay attention to the ballot boxes! Many 'bricks & mortar' establishments frequently run in-store sweepstakes/ contests, and surprisingly, not that many people usually enter. Even if there are 50 or so entries - your odds are still exceptionally good!

2. 'Crinkle' your entries.

The rationale behind this is that if your entry is all 'scrunched' up (instead of just a smooth/flat piece of paper), then it increases your chances of winning when someone makes a draw. This is simply because it would be 'easier' to grab onto this type of entry, than say a flat, smooth piece of paper that could slip through your fingers.

3. Carry business cards with you for a 'free lunch'!

It is a great way to win a lot of free lunches and dinners! Plus, what is even BETTER is it doesn't have to cost you anything! There are online 'business' card services which will print 'free' business cards for you. One service I am aware of is called 'VistaPrint' which will print 250 cards "free" for you. (I put it in quotes - because it is 'kinda' free. When you pick something you like, and go to get them shipped, they will have a whole bunch of "upgrade" options to get you to buy something, and then when you skip past all of that, they will print their logo on the back of your business card but give you the option of 'removing' it for 'only' about $5. And finally, if you do just choose to opt-in with the 'free' cards, you will pay about $5 in shipping charges for a 3-week delivery). HOWEVER... It is an inexpensive way to save yourself a ton of time - think of it as '250 entry forms' that you don't have to write by hand - and you can look pretty classy when you enter.

4. Go to strip malls/outdoor malls/etc.

A lot of people go to big malls because they are convenient, which means that sometimes the 'smaller' strip malls don't get as much walk in traffic. They still oftentimes have sweepstakes / ballots, but not as many people enter, meaning you have a better chance of winning. PLUS - big bonus! :) You are getting exercise! (I know for me sometimes it is too easy just to sit in front of a computer, so if I have a good excuse to get up and walk around, then this helps!)

5. Join Loyalty Programs

Almost every major department store, major chain, etc, etc, has some kind of 'regular' sweepstakes running for people who have taken the time to sign up for their 'loyalty' cards. Plus, usually you will get something 'free' like air miles, etc. (In fact, I was recently walking through an airport, and someone stopped me and told me that if I signed up for a Visa card right then and there, that they would give me 15,000 'free' airmiles, which apparently is worth about $600 for a flight! I didn't do it then, but now I am thinking that maybe I should have!)

Now - I don't recommend buying up a bunch of stuff "just" to get an entry. BUT, if you are going to be buying something 'anyways', then you may as well use a loyalty card at the same time. You can then accumulate points for things like trips, merchandise, etc, and usually every 2-3 months, if not sooner, there will be some kind of sweepstakes offered. (As an aside - if you are wondering how the companies benefit - they generally use the data/purchasing habits to determine which products sell well, which don't, and so forth. Consequently, it actually helps their business grow as well. They analyze your purchasing habits as well as many other customers, together, in order to come up with this information). Bottom line, if you like to buy from a particular store, then you may as well get their customer loyalty card!

BONUS TIP: For this tip, while not 'technically' a sweepstakes - many smaller mom & pop shops will have 'in-store' customer loyalty cards as well. They don't always publicly display it (i.e., you have to ask), but when you do - they will take your name

Secret 'bonus' referral strategy – how you can increase your chances of winning

I was very impressed when I saw this. There is a lady, who maintains a Facebook page, with a list of 'WooBox' sweepstakes. (Simply do a Google search for 'Woobox sweepstakes', and you should see it in the Top 10 listings). It starts off saying "HUGE LIST OF WOOBOX SWEEPSTAKES TO ENTER..."

The 'smart' thing is that in each of the links she has – every time someone clicks on one of the entries, she gets a 'bonus' referral entry, thus increasing her chances of winning prizes significantly.

I think this is a very smart strategy, because (a) she gets good chances of winning prizes, and (b) the companies holding sweepstakes benefit from increased exposure, making it a more successful promotion.

So how do you benefit? Find a list of 'referral' based sweepstakes that give you bonus entries, create a Facebook page for it titled something like 'WIN CAR SWEEPSTAKES!' or 'WIN CASH SWEEPSTAKES', with a list of sweepstakes. When people do a Google search, they are likely to find your list, enter, and then you can enjoy your increased bonus entries, and increased chances of winning!

and record your purchases. Every 'x' number of purchases you
will usually get a 'free' item. (I used to go to this small
restaurant in town for breakfast. Every '5th' breakfast I would
get free - which was really nice! But I had to explicitly ask them
about it. I think I had only noticed it one day simply because
someone else was getting their name entered into a book one
time when I went to pay, and I asked what that was all about.
And it paid off! :))

6. Look for 'instant' wins

Now this I do have to attribute to a T.V. program I saw called
'High Stakes Sweepstakers'. It was a pilot episode talking about
sweepstaking, and they were profiling various successful
sweepstakers. What I thought was fascinating was this. There
was a family that – when they went to buy groceries – would
explicitly search for products that offered 'instant wins'. Now
while the way they were doing it may have not been the
healthiest diet (they bought a lot of candy & soda), I can see
how they could get some nice wins in the long run. They were
just simply playing the odds – and if you purchase enough
products with instant win prizes – you are bound to win
something!

(In fact, I remember as a kid, I really liked Hostess Chips... That
was because they had a promotion whereby if you bought a
bag, you could win many different things like a new bag of
chips, and other prizes... I ended up buying a few bags of chips,
and was always excited when I found I got a 2nd bag for free...
And – lo and behold – MANY years later – here I am, in a book,

remembering the brand name 'HOSTESS' – and telling you about it! How is that for marketing and its effectiveness? :))

But I do admit... You can get some nice instant wins from products like that, and it is pretty thrilling when you do so.

How to Win Cash and Prizes by Playing Computer Games

While not really a sweepstakes, but more of a contest -- it is possible to win cash and prizes simply from playing computer games. It is very, very, very hard -- and the odds that you'll win are very low. But, if you or someone you know loves to play computer games – then why not try and win while playing at the same time. (This can be really useful if you have a son, daughter, grandson and granddaughter that loves computer games, and just can't get away from them!)

Some of the most popular computer games as of this writing, are League of Legends and World of Warcraft. (You can find a list of other online games that a lot of people play, from here: http://www.mmorpg.com/) . However, since there are so many people playing these computer games, it is almost like competitive sports. Everyone might want to play basketball and be in the NBA, but only a few people will ever make it.

In 2012, League of Legends (http://na.leagueoflegends.com/news/league-legends-season-two-feature-5-million-prize-pool) was offering a $5 million prize pool for people playing the computer game. However, to give you an idea of the odds -- just to even be considered for entry --

you would have to play about 200 hours of computer games. (This translates to working at a job, 8 hours a day, for five weeks straight). At that point, you would probably have to play another 200-300 hours to get a "high ranking", in order to form a team for competitive play. Once you've played about 500 hours of this computer game, and only if you are skilled at it, may you move on and compete against other players. But, if you are going to be playing computer games *anyway*, and you have some talent, you may as well see if you can win some prizes while you are at it!

It kind of reminds me of the comic strip "The Far Side" by Gary Larson from the 1980s and 1990s. Millions of children were addicted to playing Super Mario Brothers from Nintendo. Gary Larson created this cartoon, joking that perhaps one day children could get a job from playing computer games. Little did he know this would become a reality many years later. (You can actually get a job as something called a 'game tester', which many times can actually pay upwards of $50-$60k/year).

I wanted to include the cartoon here and contacted the Gary Larson representatives (the author of the Far Side series). However, he only licenses his cartoons to 'academic' publications. So until this book becomes an academic publication, and you can study about sweepstakes in college or university, you'll need to do a Google search for something called "Hopeful Parents – Gary Larson" and view it online. Take a look and see! You'll really enjoy the cartoon!

Virtual World Prizes

It is also possible to make or win cash from virtual worlds. These tend to be online communities where people talk to each other ('chat'), in the form of a computer game. One of the more popular ones is called Second Life.

It is a complete sub-culture, with its own rules and regulations. As an aside – while not a sweepstakes – a woman named Ailin Graef made worldwide headlines in 2006 when she "made" $1,000,000 from playing the computer game. She was a virtual 'real-estate' baron in the Second Life game. (http://en.wikipedia.org/wiki/Anshe_Chung)

How to Get Companies to Offer More Prizes to Increase Your Chances of Winning

Companies decide whether to spend more money on 'prizes', or more money on 'advertising' (T.V., radio, internet, mobile, etc) based on which method gives them more long-term sales. You can influence their decision on which one to do.

"Split Testing" is a marketing term used to describe when a company tests one type promotion, versus another, to determine which one is more effective at generating sales. Many larger companies, have very sophisticated systems set up, where they can measure the exact effectiveness of a promotion. With most sweepstakes being entered online, or through mobile devices nowadays -- they can measure *exactly* how many people come to the promotion page, how many people enter, and how many people make a purchase. They know the exact number.

Winner's Circle!

"I just recently won a large sweep from IGN $4,000 plus some t shirts and a bar of soap. I was ecstatic." – Betty S.

Likewise, if a company runs a Super Bowl ad, or makes a YouTube video commercial, they can also see how many people view it, how many people share it, and -- how many resulting sales there are.

After doing this split testing, they can decide whether or not they want to do more TV commercials, or give away more prizes. The cool thing is, is that you can actually make a difference -- and increase the likelihood that they will give away more prizes instead of making TV commercials. How you do this is by simply telling friends and family about the promotion, especially if you think they have good products or services. The company will be able to measure how many people get exposed to their marketing message -- and if it is greater for sweepstakes, and they make money -- then you can be very sure that they will be running a promotion with prizes for you to win, again, again, and again.

How to Get Companies to Give You Extra Prizes Because They 'Like' You

Judging agencies are basically people or organizations that are responsible for hosting the sweepstakes. These people verify that the sweepstakes are run fairly, and that the winner(s) receive their prizes. Many times, for smaller companies – it is the company itself that acts as a judging agency. For larger companies – they tend to use 3rd party companies that all they do is host and manage sweepstakes. Funny thing is – many people do not realize that you can actually increase your chances of winning – or simply get '2nd drawing' prizes – by what you say and what you do, when you correspond with a judging agency. Following is a list of what you can do.

Tip: How to keep yourself going if you encounter a 'dry' spell

Sign up for freebies or samples. There are many companies that are willing to send you samples of products. And it's like a mini prize for yourself. As a matter of fact, my mother signed up for a sample pack for me from a website called SampleSource.com. I admit, that it was nice to receive a couple chocolate bars in the mail, as well as soaps and shampoos. There are a number of different websites like this, and you can just do a search in many search engines such as "product + sample". So for example, you might type in "tide detergent sample" to get a sample of Tide detergent!

1. Always treat sponsors with respect, even if your prize is not delivered on time.

Sometimes prizes get lost in the mail. Or sometimes there's miscommunication between departments, and the prize doesn't get sent out in first place. If this happens, be patient. I know it is very exciting to win a prize, but don't badger the sponsor. Because otherwise, you could possibly disqualify yourself from future sweepstakes with that company.

For example, we were working with one company, and two of the prizes did not get sent out to the winners. One woman was very, very excited, because it was the first prize she had won in her life. Another woman, from what I could tell, entered many different sweepstakes, and was used to winning. Both sent in e-mails, asking where the prizes were. The first woman was very understanding, while the second was very belligerent. Surprisingly, the one that was belligerent was the one who was used to winning a bunch of different prizes. The woman who never won before, was very polite in her correspondence. Of course, she was upset that she had not received anything yet, but she was very respectful.

Of course the situation got resolved, the sponsor was contacted, and the prizes were sent out. But the woman that was rude in her correspondence, will <u>never</u> have a chance to win from future sweepstakes with that company, because she was put on a 'ban' list, and banned from any and all future promotions. The one that was polite and respectful, in addition to her regular gift, was sent a bonus gift as a way of saying thank you for being patient. And, of course, she can enter future sweepstakes and still has a chance of winning those too.

So always be respectful when corresponding with sponsors. They are people too!

2. Always send follow-up letters/thank-you notes to the company that sent you a prize.

There are a bunch of different reasons why you want to do this. One, it is just good manners. Two, sponsors decide whether or not they're going to run sweepstakes in the future partially based on the response that they get from the current sweepstakes. So when you send them a thank-you note, it makes them feel good, tells them that they are getting results, and therefore they are more likely to run future sweepstakes. Finally, one of the biggest things is that it could result in bonus prizes for you.

For example, from time to time a company will have extra prizes. Whether it was because not enough people entered the sweepstakes, or whether it was because someone declined the prize, they do have extra prizes. Ssometimes finding a new winner can be a lot of work. This is simply because, you might need to contact them, verify that their address is correct, get an affidavit, and so forth.

However, if they have a good relationship with someone that has won before, sometimes they will send that extra prize as a bonus prize to the winner.

In fact, we (SweepersChoice) have done that from time to time. A couple times, we went through several iterations of trying to find a potential winner. The 'potential' winners needed to fill in an affidavit, and send it back to us within a certain time frame, but didn't. Subsequently, we had several extra prizes. We decided to award them to previous winners who had sent us thank-you notes, and appreciated the work we had done in the past.

3. Be grateful for any prizes you do receive, even if they are really, really, small.

You should always be grateful for any prize you receive, even if it is not what you wanted. One big reason is simply because sponsors do put a lot of time and effort into making this a successful and fun promotion for all the participants. The second reason is that it is just simply good manners, and goo karma.

For example one time, when we were selecting some potential winners, two of the prizes were declined. One woman was very grateful, but mentioned that she was heading out on a vacation, and would not have the time to fill in the necessary affidavits to claim her prize. She thanked us, and asked that the prize be awarded to someone else. This was perfectly fine.

Another woman, instead of being grateful, complained because the prize value was too small and it was not what she wanted. So she snubbed her nose, and told us to award it to someone else simply because this prize was "beneath" her. Of course we awarded the prize to someone else. However, she is now banned from any and all future promotions.

One thing that you need to remember is that sweepstakes are run by companies to increase their exposure and increase their market presence. Quite simply, companies choose to either use paid advertising, or offer consumers a chance to win prizes through sweepstakes. They want good publicity. If someone is selected as prize winner, they want someone who will be happy with it because then that person will be happy when they tell other friends and family and so forth. Make sure you are polite and respectful. Besides, if you're grateful -- there's always the possibility that the grand prize winner may not be able to claim their prize, and if you are a runner-up, you might get it yourself!

Winner's Circle!

"I am the one that won $10,000 on the "Hostess" sweepstakes... The suggestion I have is consistency and never give up and set time out of everyday to enter contests. I was in shock when I received the phone call from Hostess... He did not send me an email... He called and asked me to open up my computer and he sent me the email while I was on the phone with him. The conversation started out "Not many people receive phone calls like this one you are receiving"... "You have just won our grand prize of $10,000 in our summer baseball sweepstakes at Hostess"... I also win lots of other prizes... About every couple of weeks I win something. I have won so many prizes that I can't list them all... at least 70-100... I have been sweeping for about 2 years and am still dedicated to it..." – Karen K.

4. Enter according to the frequency specified.

Some sweepstakes will specify that you can only enter once per day, once per week, once per month, or just once. Other sweepstakes will specify that you can only enter once per household.

Some people think that they can game the system, by using different e-mail accounts but for the same person. But the technology exists to very easily detect that, and disqualify any abuse.

Most companies will be forgiving if it seems to be an honest error. However, if it seems that someone is deliberately creating hundreds of different accounts to simply game the system, they will very easy disqualify those additional entries, and maybe even the individual.

How to Get Prizes Simply by Talking About Companies

Tell Friends, Family, and Online Social Connections About the Promotion

<u>Sponsors pay attention to how successful a particular promotion is.</u> From time to time, if they notice a specific individual really doing a fantastic job of promoting their sweepstakes, they might award them a bonus prize as a way of saying thank you.

As matter of fact, there is actually a company called "Klout" that does precisely this. People who seem to have a strong online presence, or more specifically can influence the opinions of their friends, are awarded special perks and bonuses. This particular company works with a bunch of different organizations to award those bonuses.

Likewise, if a sponsor notices an individual working hard to promote sweepstakes, they might give them a bonus prize just for 'helping' out. So who knows, if you're a fantastic marketer, you might even get a job – if you want one!

Power of the "Right" Thinking

I thought I would make a comment about this. A lot of people have heard of the power of the thinking "good" thoughts, but don't really *understand* it. Nor do they understand how to use it correctly.

Thinking good thoughts is not simply a matter of saying that "I think I am going to win a prize, I think I am going to win a prize, I think I'm going to win a prize". It is about opening yourself up to existing opportunities, and learning how to recognize them.

For example, let's say you have two women. The first one is very pessimistic, and doesn't believe that she can win anything. She is absolutely correct. The second woman, has a very optimistic outlook on life. She believes she can win, and win a lot, and she is *also* absolutely correct. Let's say both women have university age children, and walk into a car dealership. Both notice a contest going on, but see that in the rules it says that you need to be under 30 to participate.

The first woman, who is very pessimistic -- might look at this contest, and then think to herself "Wow, here is another stupid contest that I can't enter because of age requirements. That's just so unfair." So, she walks out of the dealership, angry that she can't participate. The second woman, on the other hand, realizes of course that she's too old to participate. But, she knows she has university age children, so calls one of them up, and tells them to get their butt down to the dealership to try and win a car. She has an agreement with her children to share prizes that she wins. Since the children know their mom is a winner, and somehow she just "magically" seems to win a lot, they are agreeable and show up at the dealership. And wouldn't you know it, it just so happens to be her lucky day. One of her children enters and wins the contest, and a few weeks later, her family is now the proud new owner of a new car.

Both women were too old to participate. But one had the "right" thinking, and found out how she could participate regardless. The other didn't, and subsequently never had a chance. Who do you want to be?

When you are entering sweepstakes, you need to believe in yourself, and believe that you can win. Yes, it is a game of chance, but the more you enter, the better your chances of winning. Can you imagine what the world would be like if the first time a man asked a woman out on a date, he was rejected, and he gave up? What it would be like? There would be no marriage, no babies -- and there wouldn't be anybody to write this book or even read it!

You need to be open to the possibility of winning, believe that you can win, and <u>then</u> actively search out those opportunities and find out how you can participate. Then, of course, just do it!

Although I've already made my point, I'd like to share a funny joke I heard a long time ago.

There was a man and he really wanted to win the lottery. Every night he would pray to God that he could win, and every morning he would wake up with no winnings. Finally, exasperated, the man shouted out to God, "Why won't you let me win?" A voice boomed out from the sky saying "If you want to win, at the very least buy a ticket!"

Moral of the story -- you can't win anything if you don't enter!

Secret Strategy - How 'Socializing' the 'Right' Way Can Get You Free Prizes

In a nutshell – if you say good things about a company, and people listen, then you can get free gifts and prizes. Companies employ third party companies to monitor what people say about them. If they seem to have 'influence', then they will tend to win the favor of the person with influence.

One of the most popular (yet unknown amongst mainstream users) is a company called "Klout.com". This was one of the first companies to start the electronic, behind the scenes, monitoring to give out 'perks' or 'prizes' because of an individuals 'influence'. The strategy is not new, but the way they do it, is.

What they do is use an algorithm to determine how 'influential' people are within social media. If they get a certain "score" (kind of like your 'credit' score, but instead it measures your 'influence' on the internet), then they will send this information to companies. Those companies then tend to send you free gifts/perks/etc in order to win your favor.

This is an example of what I have heard from a few people, and read in stories on the internet. I do not know how accurate it is

– I am simply passing this information on to you. According to these stories, this is what has happened and does happen. Let's say you are going on a vacation to Las Vegas. You tell all your Facebook and Twitter friends, and then they start telling all their friends. You have good 'influence', because you can get other people to talk about what you are doing. Companies doing this type of internet monitoring would then see that you have influence and perhaps notify certain companies, such as airlines and hotels, in Las Vegas. You board the plane, and wouldn't you know it, it's your lucky day! You get a free upgrade to first class. You are excited and tell all your friends on Facebook & Twitter, about what a great airline "XYZ" Airlines are. You then check into your hotel, and again, wouldn't you know it, it's your lucky day *again*! You get an upgrade to a penthouse suite because they just 'happened' to have one available! You again tell your friends on Facebook & Twitter, and other social media about what a great company XYZ hotels are!

Taken directly from the Klout.com website (as of May 2013):

"We use more than 400 signals from eight different networks to update your Klout Score every day.

The majority of the signals used to calculate the Klout Score are derived from combinations of attributes, such as the ratio of reactions you generate compared to the amount of content you share. For example, generating 100 retweets from 10 tweets will contribute more to your Score than generating 100 retweets from 1,000 tweets. We also consider factors such as how selective the people who interact with your content are. The more a person likes and retweets in a given day, the less each of those individual interactions contribute to another person's Score. Additionally, we value the engagement you drive from unique individuals. One-hundred retweets from 100 different people contribute more to your Score than do 100 retweets from a single person."

They then go on to say this:

"Perks are exclusive rewards you earn for your influence. Every day, influencers receive amazing products, discounts and VIP access that is only available to Klout users.

All you have to do is be yourself. Perks are given to you based on a variety of things, including where you live, your influential topics, or your Klout Score. Don't miss out! Check back every day to see if you've earned a Klout Perk."

So basically this means that if you have a lot of friends on Facebook & Twitter, and if you then post something, and those friends 'talk' about it (i.e., share it, retweet it, etc), then you will have a good 'Klout' score. The more people in your 'friends' list (or followers), and the higher the percentage of people talking about it, the higher your score will be. From the Klout site, you may also 'redeem' your "perks" based on your influence.

From what I've heard, people 'start' to notice free gifts, etc, when they get a score of around 60. Obviously, the higher you get, the more likely you are to get bigger and better prizes & gifts.

Aside – the 'dark' side:

As an aside though – there is a little bit of a 'dark' side to this… While people have been known to get 'free' hotel upgrades, free car rental upgrades, and so forth – they don't necessarily 'know' they are getting it because of their 'influence'. They figure 'Gosh, that company is really nice!'

In reality, the company is hoping that the person will go onto Twitter/Facebook/etc, and tell all their friends what a great company it is. What is a bit 'dark' about this is the fact that it could be considered 'subtle' manipulation… The person receiving these free gifts does not

Winner's Circle

"My first win was a trip to Hollywood and winning it was a complete fluke. I knew nothing about entering sweepstakes; but I received an e-mail asking you to predict who would win the Oscars. I had not seen one of the movies, but decided to try my luck. About a week later I received an [affidavit] stating I had won. My husband did not believe it and thought it was just a publicity stunt. I sent the affy back and my husband and I went to Hollywood for 5 wonderful days with all expenses paid, plus going to the head of the line at all events with a special escort. Needless to say, I got hooked on sweeping and have won some wonderful prizes over the past 7-8 years; the latest being an all expense trip to London for four." – Doris C.

'know' they are receiving them because of their influence.

But, now you know. And as G.I. Joe would say, "knowing is half the battle!" So if you start receiving a bunch of free gifts in the mail, or notice you start getting bumped up to first class on those trips, you know why that might be. (And if you don't know who G.I. Joe is, and are reading this, then oh my! Go watch some TV! :) And then enter sweepstakes!).

How to Get Free Products and Prizes in Exchange for Promoting Sponsors

Companies are always looking for different ways of promoting their products and services. In fact, from time to time, I offered a couple of free licenses in exchange for someone to be doing an honest review of the software. Generally speaking, if you want something free, you should offer to do something in exchange for that.

Mommy Blogs

While this is a little bit of work to get set up, there are lots of women doing this, and getting free products in the process. Basically, they set up an online blog and do product reviews for companies. They might contact companies individually, they might hear about it through Web forms, but they do a product review. I have seen many women get anything from books, to cooking items, to household items -- to whatever it is they want, in exchange for doing a review. And, they probably get $300-$400 worth of merchandise a month. So, if you have a little bit

Stealth Tactic - Radio/Call-In Sweepstakes

Now this is an interesting, stealth tactic to increase your chances of winning. I don't necessarily recommend it, because in some ways I don't feel it's in the 'spirit' of what sweepstakes were intended for, but I thought it would include it so you're aware of what some people do indeed do to win prizes.

I was talking with a few hard-core sweepers, and was surprised to learn that they used such tactics. All of them had a favorite radio station, and from time to time that radio station would be giving away prizes. And there were four or five women in this club. So, if one of the radio stations was giving away a prize -- the woman listening to it would text all her friends and tell them to phone and try to win the prize.

If one of them got through, she would accept the prize, then send it to the friend that wanted that particular prize. And they would take turns, sharing prizes.

Doing this, all five women essentially increased their chances of winning in any given sweepstakes by about 25 times. One, because there were five women entering. Second, because instead of just covering one radio station, they were actually now covering five different radio stations that offered their own unique prizes.

So, this is an interesting strategy that you can use to increase your chances of winning radio/call-in sweepstakes.

of free time, and if you're interested in this kind of thing, then I recommend doing that.

A few things though:

(a) Always provide an honest review of the product. Yes, companies want you to say that it is the most amazing thing since sliced bread. However, if you are reviewing a number of different products -- and every review says exactly the same thing, it becomes pretty obvious that you're not sincere, and you are just saying it to get free products. And long-term, your readers will value <u>honest</u> reviews, as will potential sponsors. And you can believe that potential sponsors check out your website if you're asking them for products.

(b) Network with other women. There are a number of online forums -- not just sweepstakes forms -- where women discuss product reviews. You can look this up in pretty much any search engine and find details.

(c) Conduct fair drawings. Many times a company will send you two products, one for yourself to review, and one to give away as a prize. Unfortunately, some women pretend to give away a prize honestly, when all they do is give it to friends and family. The first time you do this, maybe no one will ask. The second time, maybe you'll get lucky again. But, if you start to develop any kind of following -- it will become really obvious. And if it becomes this obvious, then it really hurts your reputation, and people will not want to deal with you in the future.

One thing that is really, really, funny, is that I know of two women who are both very well known within the sweepstakes community. One is very well respected, and it is obvious that she's very successful financially. The second, while well known for all her prize winnings, and people listen to her, they don't really respect her or do business with her. She actually asked me one time how she could improve her business, and although I told her, I don't think she really "heard" me. Subsequently, she is still jealous of this other woman and still just trying to make ends meet.

The difference between the two is how they conduct themselves online and off-line. The first woman is very generous, and is very genuine about helping other people. When you read her blog, it is obvious that she's trying to help you find good prizes for you to win. Subsequently, people do business with her and she is very successful. The second woman, while she has a very professional online presence -- it is all about herself. Sure, she might help someone here and there, but it is obvious that she cares only about "numero uno". And that she is focused on how to increase her prize winnings only. Subsequently, people will listen to her – because she gets in their 'face' so to speak – but they don't really do business with her. And she doesn't quite understand why.

So bottom line, if you're going to conduct any kind of online drawings, do them fairly. Long-term, this will benefit you, and you will enjoy a lot of success.

Video reviews

There are also a number of YouTube channels that get a lot of free products simply for doing online video reviews. One of the most popular and obviously successful types of channels happens to be with young women reviewing cosmetic products. If you love cosmetics, then this is something you should look into. I've noticed the successful ones tend to be those that show you how you can use cosmetics to look like popular celebrities such as Lady Gaga, Britney Spears, or Rihanna. Of course, you don't have to review cosmetic products, but it is one of the most popular types of review channels.

For other channels, simply do honest reviews. Now one thing to note, is that you don't have to say it's "a piece of crap" if it is (and hopefully you would not have been reviewing that type of product in first place), but you should outline its benefits and give an honest assessment of it. If you do this, eventually you will start to develop a bit of a following, and start to enjoy more success.

Stealth Tactic - Enter 'hard to enter' sweepstakes

The harder it is to enter a sweepstakes, the more likely you are to win.

I have seen countless sweepstakes where the only prize is a five dollar gift card. Yet, there are thousands of entries, and sometimes even tens of thousands -- simply because all someone had to do, was click a button. Conversely, I have seen big cash prizes ($25,000) with less than a couple hundred entries.

For example, in the 2011 "Dad's Pet Food"/"Dollar General" sweepstakes, they were sponsoring a sweepstakes where they were giving away $100,000 over the course of three months. $1,000 a day, for 90 days.

All you had to do was send in a picture of your pet with some Dad's Pet Food for a chance to win. Granted, it was a trip to the pet store, but for 30 minutes of 'work', you had a chance to win $1,000.

I sent an e-mail to my list. Within several weeks, I received 7 messages from 7 excited winners, telling me that they had each won $1,000 each.

How is that for 30 minutes of "work"?

And as an aside – 2 years later – Dollar General/Dad's Pet Food is benefitting from marketing exposure in this book, which will be seen by countless individuals for years to come!

How's that for a 'win-win-win' sweepstakes? Amazing!

Tips on how to be more successful:

a) **Inject your own personality.** Think about it. Do you like watching television that is scripted, or do you like natural spontaneous conversation? Would you prefer to watch news for the rest of your life, or funny movies? People like personality. People like controversy. People like people who have their own opinion, and can stand on their own two feet. If you're making your own channel, make it fun and make it unique. If you are a grandmother, you might call this "Granny's Product Reviews". If you're under 20s or 30s, you might call it "Stylish Girl" reviews. And if you're a mother, you might simply call it "Mummy Knows Best Reviews". Have fun with it. Make it your own.

b) **Comedy.** Try and inject some humor into your channel. People love to laugh, and I think sometimes people are way too serious. They are worried about their finances, they are worried about their family, and they are just plain worried. People like to relax and take a break -- and if you are funny, that helps them do it.

c) **Get other people on your show.** Can you imagine having a talk show, where a woman only talked about herself? A talk show where she never invited any speakers, but just talked about how great she was? While it is possible to be successful with this format, it's a heck of a lot easier if she invites friends, speakers, and other personalities. If you do this in your video channel, it helps to make it that much more interesting.

Getting Prizes from Prize Exchanges

Since more and more companies are holding some type of sweepstakes in order to promote your product or service, more and more prize exchanges are popping up. Simply put, sometimes you win something that you don't' want, and can exchange your prize with someone else's prize for something you do want. Many prize exchanges can be found in online sweepstakes forums.

For gift cards, there are online places where you can buy and sell them. In many cases, the company providing the gift card exchange marketplace will take a 10-20% cut of the face value of the card. But, if you find yourself in a situation where you really can't use it, getting 80% back in the form of cash or another gift card, as opposed to nothing, can be quite good.

Top 10 Tips to Increase Your Chances of Winning Sweepstakes

If you've read the 'SweepersChoice' strategy guide, then this section will be very familiar to you. While some parts have been modified/updated, you can move on to the next section if you wish. Otherwise, this list is a good list of what you can do to increase your chances of winning significantly.

Winning sweepstakes can be a lot of fun. My mother gets excited every time she hears the doorbell ring, and in fact some of our telephone conversations consist of her telling me what to watch for in the mail (in case she's won something for me), or what her latest or greatest prizes have been. The first time she called I admit it was a bit of fun when she was giving me gift certificates for free meals. After that, sometimes she's called to share a gift card for groceries, or just share some very cool prizes such as exclusive concert tickets.

That being said, there are a few quick and easy strategies you can employ to help increase your chances of winning, and winning more often.

1. Winning Sweepstakes is a Numbers Game.

The more you enter, and the more often you enter, the better your chances of winning. Simply put, if only two people enter a sweeps, then you have a one in two chance of winning. Or, in other words, a 50% chance of winning. If 10,000 people enter, and you only have one entry in 10,000, then your chance of winning is about 0.01%. It's still possible for you to win, but less likely.

Likewise, the number of sweepstakes you enter on a regular basis plays a big part. If you only enter one sweepstakes in a month, then it is either win or lose. But, if you enter 300 sweepstakes/month that have 100 entries each, for a total of

3,000 entries, then you are much more likely to win something, or maybe even a few prizes.

From my experience from talking with people that successfully win sweepstakes, usually as a minimum they will enter *at least* 50 different sweepstakes per day. If they want to really increase their chances, they will enter usually at least 250-300/day. (As an aside, SweepersChoice can help you achieve this easily! Check it out here!)

SweepersChoice.com

Tip: How to make new sweeping friends and increase your chances of winning more

Yahoo! Groups and Facebook groups are also a great way of sharing new contests, developing new friendships. One thing I recommend is genuinely helping other people find them enter sweepstakes that want. My mother relates the story of one woman that would "pretend" to help people. Basically, she would post a "brand-new contest" minutes before it ended, so that no one really had a chance to enter it except for her. The first couple times, people thought it was an accident. She would "pretend" that she was trying to help people, and then ask for help from them. But very quickly people started realizing what she was doing, and no one would help her. You could call that "karma". On the other hand, there have been women that have gone out of their way to help people, and then when they find themselves in a crunch -- they have tens or hundreds of people willing to vote for them in a pinch. And you tend to find these people win a lot of prizes...

Winner's Circle

"I have won some great prizes on other sweepstakes sites and also some on [this software]. I love doing sweepstakes! I have won $10,000 twice and an all expense paid trip to Egypt that was awesome. Anyways thanks for all you do for the sweepstakes!" – Cheryl

2. Enter 'Hard to Enter' Sweepstakes.

There are some companies that make it difficult for people to enter sweepstakes, such as implementing CAPTCHAs, having to create a user account, having to fill in a survey, etc, etc, before you can enter. (Personally, I feel those companies are making a mistake, because they are 'limiting' the exposure of the sweepstakes, when the goal is to get as many people to know about the company & promotion as possible). However, the good news for you is that the odds are very good, simply because not that many people enter.

For example, video and essay sweepstakes are notorious for this. I have seen countless essay & video type sweepstakes where there are only a handful of entrants, for prizes like $500 cash, laptops, computers, and much more. The odds are exceptionally good. Likewise, sweepstakes that require CAPTCHAs or surveys also give you very good chances to win prizes because not that many people want to enter, because it is too much work.

Now - why do I say that you need to 'know' what you want in this case? It is because these types of sweepstakes will take you a longer time to enter. Sometimes 10-15 minutes for only a couple. But if you are focused, and focus on those sweepstakes alone, then since you only have so much time in a day, you have a very good chance of winning the prizes you want.

3. Consistency Is Important.

Daily sweepstakes are great, and offer some wonderful prizes, but you need to enter daily in order to increase your chances. You need to enter on a regular basis to see results. Just like you didn't give up trying to learn how to ride a bike after the first try when you were a child, you shouldn't give up after only one or two sweepstakes. Consistency is important. (SweepersChoice can help you keep that consistency with the push of a button!)

4. Tell Your Friends and Family about Prize Winnings

While naturally, you would probably do that anyway, it is important to remember to mention the company. Why? How does that help your chances? Well - companies offer sweepstakes because in the long run, they want to introduce great products and services to people. One way of doing this is through "word of mouth" advertising, aka, through sweepstakes. If they get 'feedback' that they had a very successful promotion (i.e., lots of people talked about their company, ideally such that they ended up getting more sales because of it from people who wanted to purchase from them), then they are much more likely to offer those types of sweepstakes in the future, or even more. And, of course if there are more sweepstakes, then that means you have more chances to win.

5. Join a Sweepstakes Club!

There are many sweepstakes clubs across North America. They are people just like you, who want to win amazing prizes. But when you join these groups, you can get additional insight as to where the 'good' sweepstakes are, or ones you didn't hear of before, or new 'strategies' of winning.

Carolyn Wilman, of the 'ContestQueen.com', has an excellent selection of resources and sweepstaking clubs across the nation.

You can get access to it right here:

http://www.contestqueen.com/us-resources/meet-fellow-sweepers/sweepstakes-clubs/

You can also use a search engine like 'Google' to do a search for search terms like 'Sweepstakes Clubs Texas', or something along those lines.

Plus, you can make some amazing friendships!

6. Go to conventions!

One thing that has become increasingly popular is sweepstakes conventions. One of the largest ones (best promoted) happens to be held on an annual basis, and they are constantly changing the location to new cities. The URL always seems to be changing, but usually the

forums at http://forums.online-sweepstakes.com/ will have the most current convention details.

The 2013 'national' convention was held in Salt Lake City, Utah. The details are here: http://www.saltlakecityut2013.com/

The 2014 'national' convention was held in Orlando, Florida. The details here: http://www.spf25orlando.com/

The 2015 'national' convention will be held in Boston, Massachusetts. Details can be found here: http://www.sweepingboston2015.com/

There are also other conventions that are held across the country at various times.

One is the 'Michigan Spring Meeting' – run by Al Sayward, a

long time sweeper. He is famous for his love of candy – so if you go to one of his conventions, you will most likely, at the very least, win some delicious chocolate or candy!

Another one is the Pennsylvania Convention (known as the "Hershey's" convention in sweeping circles, because that is where Hershey's headquarters is located). The organizer is currently on hiatus (last one was 2013), but may be started up again in the future.

And finally, the Maryland Spring Banquet is also a popular one. http://www.mdspringbanquet.com/

There are usually another 4 or 5 conventions throughout the year at different locations within the USA and Canada. You can generally find out more about these conventions simply by talking to other sweepers.

They tend to share tips and strategies on how to win more, talk about the various companies/sponsors offering sweepstakes, plus give you an opportunity to make new friends.

One thing that will probably amaze you (if you are new to this) is the 'extent' of winning streaks some people had. Like I said in the introduction, it almost seemed like there was an 'unspoken' rule that you needed to win $25,000+ or more to attend. While of course that is not true – you can definitely learn a lot from the people that show up! Plus – you can have a lot of fun.

The conventions all tend to consist of the following. 'Prize sessions' – where literally all they do is give out prizes – just for showing up! Prizes tend to range from $25 - $500 in value. 'Nicer' ones tend to be computers, tablets, e-readers, and so forth! So if you want to have a lot of fun, then I recommend going to a convention! Speakers from different parts of the sweepstakes industry will give talks. This may include how to: increase your chances of winning, software tools to help you enter more efficiently, find corporate sponsorships, sweepstakes, and so forth. Finally, there is usually a banquet where 'grand' prize winners are announced.

Two years ago, at the Atlanta national convention – there were TWO winners for a car each. Each opted to receive the money instead, which was $15,000 USD! This year, in Salt Lake City, Utah, there was another $15,000 USD winner!

7. Use Sweepstakes Referrals!

Many sweepstakes sites will have some kind of 'tell a friend' option, or 'referral' option. You can get a lot of 'bonus' entries by calling up friends who enter sweepstakes, and making sure they add you to their list, while you add them to their list.

Then, in some cases, you can be getting two people working together, and you are only doing half the work, while having twice the fun!

8. Check Your E-mail Box and Phone Messages on a Regular, Daily Basis.

I know this goes without saying, but you would be surprised at how many people have lost out on winning really cool sweepstakes prizes just because they didn't respond in time. Many 'sweepstakes' have a 48-hour window, and if you don't reply within that timeframe, they will award it to someone else. (And in fact, recently I almost missed out on something! I was using a particular e-mail address that I use every now and then, and it just so happened I checked it that day, and I'm glad I did! Had I not, I might have missed the 48 hour window!)

9. Enter On Off-Peak Times

I was actually surprised when I found this out, but there are actually sweepstakes promotions that will award 'instant wins' at specific times of the day. (I.e., 3:43 a.m., 7:42 a.m., 12:01 p.m., etc, etc). I am not quite sure why they do that (to me it makes more sense to make it truly random, but the fact is, that is what they choose to do). And the companies that employ that strategy tend to be ones that are offering a 'large' amount of 'instant win' prizes. So, if you see any kind of sweepstakes that specifies that prizes will be awarded at specific times in the day (or more specifically, notice that it is an 'instant-win' type of sweepstakes), then read the rules. If indeed it is this type of sweepstakes, then you can enter at odd hours to help increase your chances of winning.

I actually have heard/received reports of many people winning things at 5:30-6:30 a.m. in the morning. So it would be worth trying out.

10. Smile, have fun, and have patience!

Entering sweepstakes should be fun! It is fun imagining what great or amazing prizes you could win, and of course if you do win, it is even more of a great feeling! And of course, patience is important. This is not like a 'job' where you know you will be getting a steady paycheck every two weeks. No. These are sweepstakes. Sometimes you need to wait at least two or three months before seeing results. That is because the sweepstakes may take a month before it ends, and then it may take another 2-4 weeks for the company to contact people to award the prizes. Sometimes you may not win, because you are taking a chance. It is a game of odds, but, the nice thing about this is, the more you enter, the more <u>likely</u> you are to win!

You want to keep doing it on a consistent basis, because then if you win, you will continue to have a very good chance of winning. If you only do it once or twice, (and let's say you won three months later), then you would need to start all over and most likely wait another two to three months before seeing a prize!

4. Convention Pictures

I thought it might be fun to share some of the pictures from the conventions I attended.

2012 Atlanta National Sweepstakes Convention

First off, I have to say thank-you to Sunstar GumBrand, Travalo USA, and X-Shot. They were very gracious sponsors with us at this convention.

Secondly, some of the pictures I took while there, were amazing.

I got to go on a tour of the CNN studio – the very same TV station that is seen by millions of Americans on a daily basis. I

decided to go for the 'VIP' tour because I wasn't sure when I would visit Atlanta Georgia again. It cost a little bit extra, but was worth it!

I volunteered to go read off a teleprompter in one of the demo studios they had. The tour guide was amazed I did such a great job!

Next, I visited the world

headquarters for Coca-Cola! I was amazed at the rich history they had, and how Coca-Cola had evolved over the course of a century and became the household name they are today. I even saw the safe where they kept the "secret formula" under lock and key for Coca Cola!!

Next, I got to see an amazing live ball game with the Atlanta Braves! It was so cool doing the 'Tomahawk Chop' in person that they are so famous for!

Probably about 100 sweepers all went to the ball game. Some even shared a limousine together (I think 10 people) from the hotel to the game. I wish I had heard about that, I think it would have been great fun!

Finally, the a picture of the hotel. We also had a special car, and the car colors matched perfectly with the SweepersChoice colors! We toured the city with a number of very happy sweepers, and had some amazing experiences!

2013 Salt Lake City National Sweepstakes Convention

The very first day, before the convention really 'kicked' off, two ladies were very gracious to invite me to join them. Faye, Diane, a friend of theirs and I, all went to Ogden, Utah for a day trip to go 'Indoor-Skydiving'. It was great! The first picture is of me in the train. The second is of a restaurant we stopped at. And the third is of a really cool 'Pac-Man' game that I spotted in one of the local arcades!

Both Travalo USA and Kingston Technologies were very gracious to sponsor a number of prizes.

Travalo USA sponsored TSA-Approved perfume atomizers (spray bottles), ShaveTech USB Shavers, Beauty9 products, plus a whole host of other great products! Kingston Technologies sponsored high quality USB Flash Drives and memory cards!

As luck would have it, there was <u>another</u> beautiful, blue 'SweepersChoice' mustang convertible at this convention! While it was hot and I had to wear a lot of sunscreen, it was a fun ride!

I also had the chance to do a little bit of sightseeing while in Utah, and got some amazing pictures!

Finally, one sight that was amazing was while I was driving through the Salt Plains in Utah. Someone had written 'God Bless USA' with rocks in the sand. It was by pure chance that I had pulled over to the side of the road when I noticed this. I was actually looking to take some pictures of other scenery. But I thought it was very cool, and definitely worth including here!

2014 Orlando 25th National Sweepstakes Convention

The first picture is of palm trees, one of the first things I was greeted with as soon as I landed in Orlando. We had some amazing swag that we gave away free to people, as well as special T-Shirts and Pens. We had a prize wheel you could spin to get free prizes!

The pictures below are of the 7 lucky winners of the 'Taste of a MILLIONAIRES! Lifestyle' sweepstakes, sponsored by SweepersChoice. In the first picture, everyone is entering the super stretch limousine. The second picture is a snapshot of the

disco ball in the exclusive VIP club we attended.

Here is another picture of everyone enjoying a drink at the club. Everyone had special VIP access.

Finally, this is a picture of the beautiful 2014 fully souped up Z06 Corvette Convertible. It was amazing!

5. Interviews

Many people win a lot. But some people are amazing at what they do, while others help give sweepers the opportunities to win!

This chapter includes some interviews with some amazing people. Steve – the "Travel King", having won over 200 vacations in his lifetime, discusses his perspective on sweepstakes. Ken – the "Sweepstakes Directory King" -- having organized sweepstakes in an online directory for the last 10 years, talks about his views on sweepstakes. And then Beeb – who runs her own site as well -- her 'contest' corner, has a great story to share! Roger was another great sweeper from Canada that was recommended to me. And then finally, both Walt, a video sweeper, and Carolyn McLaughlin, an editor of a popular newsletter and convention organizer, agreed to be interviewed as well!

There are literally hundreds of other people though with untold stories, as I witnessed at the Atlanta convention in 2012, and later at the Salt Lake City convention in 2013. However, I was very fortunate to be able to interview these individuals.

Enjoy what they have to share!

Interview with Steve – The Travel King!

Steve is an amazing guy... I've met him personally – but what's really amazing is HOW MANY trips he's won in his lifetime! If you thought winning a trip to Disneyland was amazing... Imagine winning TWO HUNDRED and NINETEEN trips! Yes, I was floored when I just found out how successful he's been with that. That's like winning an average of 10 trips/year, for 20 years! That would be some amazing vacation time! (Can you imagine telling your boss you needed time off EVERY month for ANOTHER vacation? ☺)

Steve was kind enough to agree to my interview request, and here is our discussion...

Q. Please tell me a bit about yourself. How did you get started entering sweepstakes? What was your first big win that got you 'hooked'? What have you won since then?

A. Like so many "old time" sweepers I got started by being intrigued by the wins reported on the back page of Contest Newsletter. My friends told me that people never win, and that got me challenged to prove to them I could indeed win. To this day, I love the challenge...that's what keeps me going.

Interestingly, my first win of any consequence was from a "25 words or less" slogan contest for Gleem toothpaste. From that contest I won a TV and VCR. Not long after that I won my first trip.... a trip for 2 to Bermuda. I was pleasantly surprised when the judging agency said it was not a problem that I had a daughter...they paid for her to go as well. I love to win trips, especially for special and unique events. At last count I have won 219 trips.

Q. What win are you most proud of?

A. It's hard to pick just one...how about something like the top 10 or so.

1. Trip for 4 for a week on a $650,000 private yacht cruising the British Virgin Islands, with our own personal captain and personal cook... just the 6 of us for a week, dropping anchor in a different bay each night.

2. Attending the Olympics in Barcelona Spain

3. Racing in a NASCAR race car on the Charlotte track against 9 other sweepers...I came in second, missed winning by 4/10 of a second. Driver Ryan Newman was my coach, giving me spotter info in my ear during the race.

4. Attending the baseball all-star game in Seattle. The week before the trip Pepsi called and told us that they had just signed a marketing deal with Oberto meats, and that since the chairman of Oberto lived in Seattle he and his wife had invited us over for dinner the night before the all-star game. So, my wife and I, along with 6 Pepsi execs, and the Oberto couple sat around and chatted all night...the Oberto chairman's wife cooked us all dinner.

5. Four days at ESPN for a behind the scenes tour and some games.

6. A trip for 4 to a Meet and Greet in Boston with Trace Atkins on his Wounded Warrior Tour. The manager of Trace's band messed up the meet and greet, so the sponsor flew the 4 of us on another trip to meet Trace at another concert in Las Vegas to make up for it.

7. A trip to Miami to visit and tour the Univision studios. While there, we were interviewed on the Spanish equivalent of Good Morning America, and then my wife and I were cast as extras in a Spanish Soap Opera.

8. A trip to Denver for the first Monday Night NFL game in their new stadium. The next morning was the 9/11 attacks...and we had an interesting trip getting home.

9. A trip to NY to spend the day with the cast and crew of Saturday Night Live, including having lunch with them, and then doing interviews with them.

10. A one-week cruise called The Malt Shop Memories Cruise along with a dozen of the rock and roll stars of the 60's, including Frankie Avalon, Leslie Gore, Little Anthony and the Imperials, etc.

Such trips to special events that are impossible to even buy are what make the hobby so special and interesting. I could go on and on...each trip has some special story or significance to it.

Q. What kind of 'sweeping' regimen do you have? (I.e., How do you go about finding out which sweepstakes to enter? How often do you enter? Do you have favorite times to enter? Etc, etc).

A. Like "everyone" else I look for sweeps for cars, but despite 30+ years entering I have yet to win one....but I keep trying. I enter for just about any/every trip sweepstakes I can find.

I'm a sweeping addict, so I make sure I enter as many sweeps as I can each day. I maintain a list of "dailies" I make sure I enter every day....even if I am on a trip...I work hard to find the time to keep entering.

I have no favorite time to enter, but I get up between 4:30 and 5 am to start my sweeping activity.

Q. Questions from readers (we sent out a newsletter and asked them to submit questions in addition to the above ones, and these were some of them)

a) How do you keep yourself motivated to keep entering?

My motivation comes from winning. Many people suggest that when a drought comes along and I get frustrated, I should take a break for a day or two (or week). That is not me. For sure I can't win if I don't enter. So, when I get into a non-winning slump, I look for even more sweeps to enter...to work my way out of the slump.

b) When 'exactly' do you enter? (i.e., Do you enter at the beginning, middle or on its last day just a few hours before the sweep is about to close.)

For online sweeps that are one entry, I enter the day I find the sweep.

For mail-in sweeps, for one entry only sweeps, I usually wait till near the end of the promotion.

c) What conventions/tradeshows/groups/etc do you take part in to increase your chances of winning?

I have attended every sweepstakes convention since 1993...it's a great way to learn, and to keep in touch with other sweepers. No matter how much I think I know, I know I can always learn something from others.

d) Do you have any recommendations on how to track your wins? (I.e., Excel spreadsheets? Any software, etc?)

I don't keep any database of my wins....that would take just too much time. I win something every 2 to 3 days, so I just save the win notices in a file for reference... and for end of the year tax considerations.

e) Any tips on finding 'local' sweepstakes?

No real tips...I just know there are lots of local sweeps out there, so I use every method available...walk around malls, read local newspapers, check all the local TV and radio stations web sites, get all the local supermarket flyers, use online search terms that define a local sweeps, etc.

Q. What kinds of tools/websites/resources do you use to enter Sweepstakes?

A. Besides checking in at a good number of online sweepstakes newsletter/directory web sites, I make time each day to do my own Google searches.

Q. What one 'secret' tip that few people know about, could you share with people to help them increase their chances of winning?

A. I have no secret tips that I can think of. I just follow the philosophy that the more sweeps I can enter, the more chances I have to win. I find a way to make sure I enter a few hundred dailies a day, plus as many one-time only ones I can find each day.

I do spend almost all my time on what I might call high value prizes. I do not spend my time entering for CDs, DVDs, movie tickets, books, $100 gift cards, etc. Yes, it is nice to win them when I miss winning the grand prize, but I would rather spend my time trying to win the "big one." That does mean, however, that I won't win many of the smaller, but nice things, my sweeping friends win. It means that I "strike out" a lot trying for the big ones, but after 30 years of entering and winning, that's just my way.

Q. Anything else you think might be interesting to people reading this?

Using my trip wins, and the miles and hotel nights I win, I am able to take my wife on a trip once a month. She loves to travel and feels that once a month is all she wants to do.

There have been times when we have been fortunate to win trips back to back... we had a ball a few years ago when we won and had to take 6 trips over an 8 week period... that was fun for me, but very stressful for my wife. To me, the more trips the merrier, especially the international ones.

Interview with Ken – Head of SweepsAdvantage.com

Ken is a really cool guy... I've corresponded with him quite a few times over the years, and he has some good insights into sweepstakes as well!

Q. Please tell me a bit about yourself. How did you get started entering sweepstakes? What was your first big win that got you 'hooked'? What have you won since then?

A. We (Ken and Diane) live in FL now but we were born in Mass, then moved to NH then finally to FL. Our life sort of revolves around our daughter.

The first big win was an arcade version of Sony Playstation created by Pepsi. It was the size of a pinball machine and it came in a box the size of a refrigerator.

Since this win we've won a trip to rome, jewelry, many electronics including laptops, iPads, many gift cards and checks/cash.

Q. You also run the website SweepsAdvantage. Can you tell me a bit about that? (How did you get started? What's some of the most interesting stories you've read about on your forums? Why should people come to SweepsAdvantage (i.e., benefits/friendships/etc)?

My wife and I are owners of a leading Sweepstakes Directory called "Sweepstakes Advantage". I have always been heavily involved in high tech and have worked for several large technology companies. My wife Diane was an office manager.

The birth of our daughter changed things in our lives and we decided to start a business. Diane had always been a sweepstakes enthusiast starting before 1997. We combined what we knew about sweepstakes and technology.

Q. What win are you most proud of?

We've had bigger wins but because of the timing I would have to say the arcade Sony Playstation. (Our neighbors were wondering what was in the huge box).

Q. What kind of 'sweeping' regimen do you have? (I.e., How do you go about finding out which sweepstakes to enter? How often do you enter? Do you have favorite times to enter? etc).

You have to try and enter daily. It's always about the odds and the more you enter the better your odds of winning are. It's fun to enter sweepstakes that are running for 1 day only.

Q. Questions from readers (we sent out a newsletter and asked them to submit questions in addition to the above ones, and these were some of them).

a) How do you keep yourself motivated to keep entering?

A. Don't take winning too seriously. When you win, consider it a blessing.

b) When 'exactly' do you enter? (i.e., Do you enter at the beginning, middle or on its last day just a few hours before the sweep is about to close.)

A. I like to watch for trends. If you keep an eye on the Sweepstakes Advantage Winner's Circle you will see what people are winning. Enter those same sweepstakes for even better odds.

c) What conventions/tradeshows/groups/etc do you take part in to increase your chances of winning?

A. Sweepstakes Advantage has been a sponsor at some trade shows. This is a good way to meet other people who are into this hobby.

d) Do you have any recommendations on how to track your wins? (I.e., Excel spreadsheets? Any software, etc?)

A. Excel can be a good program. It's good to track how successful you are and at what times of the year or with what types of promotions.

e) Any tips on finding 'local' sweepstakes?

The newspaper or local magazines are always a good place or your local supermarket.

What kinds of tools/websites/resources do you use to enter sweepstakes?

- Sweepstakes Advantage www.sweepsadvantage.com
- Sweepstakes Plus www.sweepstakesplus.com
- Roboform

Q. What one 'secret' tip that few people know about, could you share with people to help them increase their chances of winning?

A. Check the "expiring soon" section on Sweepstakes Advantage and enter those sweepstakes with the fewest hits. These should have fewer total entries and better odds. Also, try entering sweepstakes that require a story or photo upload. Most people pass these by but they have great odds.

Q. Anything else you think might be interesting to people reading this?

Sweepstakes have been around for a very long time – at least 100 years. Remember in the wild west where the general store would have you guess how many jelly beans in the bottle to win? It's a free hobby that will be around forever.

Interview with the 'Contest Girl!' – Beeb Ashcroft!

I don't personally know Beeb... But when I asked some of my users whom they'd recommend I interview, her name came up a few times. So I contacted her, and she was gracious enough to agree to an interview! From what she said in the interview, she sounds like an amazing woman! Here is what she had to say:

Q. Please tell me a bit about yourself. How did you get started entering sweepstakes? What was your first big win that got you 'hooked'? What have you won since then?

A. I've always had a fascination with contests - I'll never forget the thrill when I called into a radio contest at age 10 and won a VHS tape! But I didn't seriously begin pursuing sweepstakes until 2008, when I discovered the booming arena of blog giveaways. I noticed that most of the blogs I visited to get information on coupon usage or homemaking were also hosting their own contests that would get relatively few entries compared to "National" sweepstakes. Entering these was a no-brainer, and I very quickly won a pretty Scrabble tile necklace. The rest is history!

Q. What win are you most proud of?

A. Winning $10,000 in the "Delicious Moments" video contest: http://www.contest-corner.com/i-won-the-delicious-moments-contest/

"I have some amazing news! My entry in the "Delicious Moments" contest received the most votes, and I have won $10,000!!! Click here to see my winning video. Thanks so much to all my readers for voting and spreading the word!! I can't believe it!!! I have been a "sweeper" – AKA someone who enters contests as a hobby – for a little over a year now, and I've always dreamed of winning a big prize. Persistence pays off – it really could happen to you!!

It all started back in September, when I read this post on Resourceful Mommy offering a Wal-Mart gift card & a booklet filled with free coupons to the first 75 people to send in a video. So I sent in a video, hoping to be one of the 75 and win some free coupons. Never did I dream that I would end up actually winning the grand prize! Who says clipping coupons doesn't pay off?!?!

Bonus: I submitted the video on my birthday. Best birthday present ever!

So thank you again from the bottom of my heart for your support! This is a major deal and will have great positive impact on my life. Being the frugal person that I am, lots of people are curious as to what I'll do with the winnings. My plan for right now is to put it into a savings account and then weigh up my options as to what will be the best investment. There are several possibilities – for example, anyone who has been to my house knows that there has never been a driveway here. So putting the funds towards installing a driveway (and garage, if zoning permits!) is one option. Of course, I will keep everyone posted!"

Q. What kind of 'sweeping' regimen do you have? (I.e., How do you go about finding out which sweepstakes to enter? How often do you enter? Do you have favorite times to enter? etc).

A. These days, I focus my sweeping mostly on "low entry" blog giveaways – i.e., blog giveaways which receive 200 entries or less. There are a number of resources out there for quickly locating such low entry giveaways - I have a compilation of sites listed here:
http://www.contest-corner.com/odds-of-winning/

I will also be launching my own website on this topic, http://www.lowentry.com/, this summer.

When I'm not entering low entry sweeps, I tend to focus on a specific need or desire - for example, I recently spent a week calling in local radio stations that were giving away tickets to a concert I wanted to attend. (I didn't win, but I did get on the radio!) If a birthday or holiday is coming up, I will start searching for prize categories that would make good gifts - electronics, CDs for certain bands, etc; or if I need to make a big purchase, I'll try to put it off when possible in case I can win a replacement. For instance, my desktop PC was on its last legs, so I entered a competition to win a computer. I was the winner and ended up with a brand new computer with much better specs than I could have afforded out of pocket!

I do the majority of my contest searching either on the sites I linked to above and online-sweepstakes.com (Which allows you to sort by category and ending date). As the webmaster of Contest-Corner.com, a sweepstakes database, I also get contests emailed to me every single day, which makes it even easier to spot things I want to enter!

Q. Questions from readers (we sent out a newsletter and asked them to submit questions in addition to the above ones, and these were some of them)

a) How do you keep yourself motivated to keep entering?

A. I don't have to do anything - the prizes I receive are all the motivation I need!

b) When 'exactly' do you enter? (i.e., Do you enter at the beginning, middle or on its last day just a few hours before the sweep is about to close.)

A. I like to focus on those sweepstakes which are about to expire, so I can get an idea of how many entrants there are, and thus, what my odds are and how much time I should spend entering it.

c) What conventions/tradeshows/groups/etc do you take part in to increase your chances of winning?

A. None, but I'd like to attend one!

d) Do you have any recommendations on how to track your wins? (I.e., Excel spreadsheets? Any software, etc?)

A. I use a Google doc to copy & paste my winning notifications in a running list. I bold each entry once I receive the prize, so I can keep track of anything that gets lost in the mail, although this happens infrequently. When a new year starts, I add a heading for that year and continue the list; I've kept the same ongoing list since 2008. At the end of the year, I go back through my list and make a separate OpenOffice spreadsheet of each prize's ARV, as I live in the US where prize winnings are taxable. I like keeping my list "In the cloud" so that I can access it from any computer to update it. It's simple, but it works for me!

e) Any tips on finding 'local' sweepstakes?

A. Keep your eyes peeled on local media and do Google searches for web resources in your area. For example, I believe that http://www.sweetiessweeps.com/ had a paid area listing local contests at one time. It can be trickier to locate these contests, but you are right to look for them as they do have better odds. I actually just launched http://www.britishgiveaways.com/ as a companion site to Contest Corner so that UK readers may locate sweepstakes open to them more easily.

Q. What kinds of tools/websites/resources do you use to enter Sweepstakes?

A. Websites/resources:

http://www.online-sweepstakes.com/ & this list: http://www.contest-corner.com/odds-of-winning/

Tools: Autofill forms plugin extension for FireFox (It makes filling in forms with your name and phone number more efficient - this isn't just helpful for sweeps, but any sort of registration form/free sample/coupon offer!)

Q. What one 'secret' tip that few people know about, could you share with people to help them increase their chances of winning?

Look for low entry blog giveaways! I wrote a guest post for MoneySavingMom.com to explain this: http://moneysavingmom.com/2012/10/save-money-on-christmas-gifts-by-entering-contests.html

Guest post from Beeb of Contest Corner:

"These days, it's extremely rare that I spend money out of pocket for birthday or Christmas presents. I have a variety of frugal strategies which I use to achieve this, but the most unorthodox one also happens to be one of my favorite pastimes: Entering sweepstakes or "Sweeping".

Yes, I've been able to utilize my hobby of entering contests to win a variety of great gift items over the years — everything ranging from camcorders to toys to MP3 players and more!

My "wins" have made for memorable and appreciated presents. But this isn't the result of being especially "lucky"; it's about using simple strategies to improve my odds of winning.

Here are a few tips for any novice who would like to try their hand at entering contests – and maybe even win a Christmas gift or two:

1. Think statistically.

People often dismiss giveaways thinking they'll never win anything, but this simply isn't true. If you enter consistently, odds are that one of these days you're going to win something. And if you narrow down your options to sweepstakes with fewer entries, your chances increase exponentially.

2. Increase your odds.

Did you know that there are hundreds of blogs hosting giveaways that receive 200 entries or less? I've won so many prizes by focusing my attention on giveaways with low entries. For example, I won the computer which I am typing this from in a blog giveaway that had less than 100 entries.

So how do you find these giveaways in the first place? There are a variety of websites that list "Low-entry" giveaways – my favorite is "Tight Wad" in Utah, which maintains a daily round-up of giveaways with few entries.

3. Make a plan of attack.

Head to a reputable contest directory such as Online-Sweepstakes.com, where you can filter giveaway listings by prize and type of giveaway. For example, you could quickly conduct a search for current electronic giveaways hosted on blogs. Focus your attention on contests for either products that your family would love or gift cards that you could use to buy presents.

4. Use your time wisely.

You don't need to sit around all day entering contests to win. Nowadays, I usually check out a low-entry link-up list such as the one I mentioned above, scan quickly for giveaways that I really like, and enter one or two. By focusing on more "winnable" giveaways, you make the most of your precious time.

5. Be realistic.

You are not guaranteed of any outcome when you enter giveaways, so you can't plan on anything specific. Sweeping is one tactic that I use as part of an overall frugal lifestyle to reduce my expenses, and while I can't plan for a specific prize the way I can plan for a coupon sale, using it as a part of my savings strategy has helped me save big over the years."

P a g e | 159

Q. Anything else you think might be interesting to people reading this?

Remember to think statistically with giveaways - don't enter one giveaway and get discouraged because you didn't win. Look for good odds, take advantage of all entry options and try to be consistent with your entering.

Interview with Roger Simmons

Roger's name was forwarded on to me by another woman who runs a contest site. She mentioned Roger was an avid reader and contestor/sweeper, and had contributed to her blog in the past. After interviewing him, I realized that he has had quite a bit of success so far.

He is based in Canada, so when he refers to entering a 'contest', it is the same meaning as entering a 'Sweepstakes' in the USA. One of the 'main' differences between a contest in Canda, and a sweepstakes in the USA, is that Canadians must answer a 'skill-testing' question before accepting a prize. Usually this is in the form of a simple math question.

Other than that, read on – and enjoy his interview!

Q. Please tell me a bit about yourself. How did you get started entering sweepstakes? What was your first big win that got you 'hooked'? What have you won since then?

A. My name is Roger Simmons. I am known in the Contesting world as trucker, truckerofbc and Roger. I started out contesting as most people have done in the past. I started out as a couponer looking to save money and get things for free. As a couponer, I created the first coupon "swap-meets" in Canada where people got together as a group and traded coupons in person and in a social environment.

It became so popular that meetups soon started forming in other cities across the country and Canada's National News network "CTV The National" did an interview of our group at a meet and trade function. Prior to this I had started doing contests and found that the time dedicated to doing both was equally important.

Contesting, or Sweepstaking as it is called in the U.S., allowed me to get products which were household items and items that were of higher value. Many were things that my family would use, but didn't want to stockpe 200 shampoos of which would lose their usefulness before we could ever use them.

I then started dedicating my time and efforts to Contesting full time. My first venture into Contesting was a voting related contest with a company called Powerbar Canada. It was for $5000 worth of Powerbar products. I did win this contest and I really felt bad for winning this contest. You see I was winning this contest for my son's football team,The Royal City Hyacks. But, they were a young boys team and would never use the product themselves. The second place team was the Calgary Cascades Swim Club in Calgary, Alberta. These were products that would actually be used due to the physical effort required by competitive swimmers. After winning this, I donated half of the $5000 in products to the Calgary Cascades and half went to the Royal City Hyacks who traded the Powerbar products for

Football related equipment. In the end it was a triple win situation. Both teams got product and I felt good with my generosity.

Since that inception, I have won so many things I cannot even remember them all. As a short list though here are some of the things I have won.

- Ladies diamond necklaces (4x) with a retail value of about $10,000
- $5000 in Powerbar food products
- $2500 Diamond tennis bracelet
- $2000 in Presidents Choice gift cards (Loblaws)
- 20x + Bulova watches with 16 being won in one contest alone
- Cash of which I have won more than $1000 in a single contest
- Multiple gift cards ranging in value from $5 to $100
- 52" Samsung TV with a Samsung Blu-Ray player and a Samsung 7-piece home stereo system
- Hoover vacuum cleaners
- Obus prize form packs (pillow, massagers, backpacks)
- Bissell steam cleaners
- 2 Ipod Nanos
- Blackberry Curve Cell Phone
- Nintendo DS
- Go Pro Hero Camera
- Sony Bloggie
- Keurig coffee

- Nestea for a year (52 certificates for free Nestea Ice Tea 12 packs)
- Movie gift certificates
- Blender
- Coffee mugs, T-Shirts, socks, underwear, shoes
- 2x Sony S Picture Frame
- T-Fal pot and pan set
- Uniball pens, Shaeffer pens
- Weedeater

These are just some of the items I have won in the last 5 years

Q. What kind of 'sweeping' regimen do you have? (I.e., How do you go about finding out which sweepstakes to enter? How often do you enter? Do you have favorite times to enter? etc).

A. My Contest regimen is very simple. I have a strong network of contesting friends that I have met over the years. Through them, my newsfeed on Facebook is filled with the latest and best contests to enter. Consistently I learn about new contests to enter each and every day along with ones that are called dailies. Although some people prefer to bookmark and make note of contests to enter each day, I prefer to just enter them as I see them. As far as entering times, I prefer to test instant win contests shortly after midnight in my time zone otherwise I have no time bias except to just get my entry in regardless. I enter contests on a daily basis since the essence of contesting is the more times you enter, the better the odds, and if you're not in it, you can't win it. Those are my two favorite sayings by which to live.

Q. Questions from readers (we sent out a newsletter and asked them to submit questions in addition to the above ones, and these were some of them)

Q. How do you keep yourself motivated to keep entering?

A. I have had times when I just have not won anything for a couple of months at a time. During these times it is easy to give up hope, but I keep on trying. I keep entering and I utilize my contesting friends for my "[complaining] that I never win attitude". At the same time if they are having a down period, we feed off each others' misery to keep us going. Generally a win will come and it will be enough to keep me going again.

Q. When 'exactly' do you enter? (i.e., Do you enter at the beginning, middle or on its last day just a few hours before the sweep is about to close.)

A. When I enter contests, I enter in order to be entered. I have no set time. I have no set period of making it a close call or just barely getting in an entry. Many times contests are based on if you get in early and your friends see it you will get credit and an extra entry if they see you entered it and enter through your link. Thus I try to get in early but for me, it is no big deal if I miss out on a contest. I just move forward to the next one.

Q. What conventions/tradeshows/groups/etc do you take part in to increase your chances of winning?

A. I do not attend any conventions or meetings for contesters, but I have met plenty of contesters in real life through my friends on Facebook. I try to make it a point to get to know each and every one of them on a personal level so that I know they are real persons and not some fictitious account set up to win under false pretenses.

Q. Do you have any recommendations on how to track your wins? (I.e., Excel spreadsheets? Any software, etc?)

A. I track my wins by photographing everything. I then place my photos on Facebook and share with all my contest friends. I also keep a copy of the picture on a USB stick. I also keep a copy of the winning email for insurance purposes. It has come in handy as our house was broken into last year and I was robbed of almost $6000 in previous prizes I had won. Our house insurance paid it back to me based on the emails and prize descriptions from the various sponsors.

Q. Any tips on finding 'local' sweepstakes?

A. For contests I use Google and Yahoo Keyword searches with the word "contest". I get any email that surfaces on the internet with the word 'contest' in it. Of course I also keyword my name in case a win comes up that I may have overlooked.

Q. What kinds of tools/websites/resources do you use to enter Sweepstakes?

A. I use places called Online Sweepstakes and I am a member of various Facebook pages setup to notify people of the latest contests. It is through these forums that many contesters share their latest find.

Q. What one 'secret' tip that few people know about, could you share with people to help them increase their chances of winning?

Many contests allow the entry of multiple UPC codes. When a contest allows this, I enter as many as I can. There are few who take the time to do this except to get in one entry. An example is the Schneiders Traditions contest. Contestants are allowed to enter each product UPC a maximum of 4x a week. Schneiders has about 65+ UPC codes and therefore is about 260 entries in a week. Another tip is to check each email. It may look like Spam but it may have a winning name enclosed. Not every email will say "congratulations".

Interview with Walt Arnett

I personally met Walt most recently at the Sweepstakes Convention in Utah. He was invited to speak because he has had tremendous success with video sweepstakes.

Here is what he had to share.

Q. Please tell me a bit about yourself. How did you get started entering sweepstakes? What was your first big win that got you 'hooked'? What have you won since then?

A. I first started entering sweepstakes after I watched an Oprah episode where she talked about someone who entered sweepstakes all the time.

They had won a bunch of prizes including a brand new truck and a boat. I wasn't 18 yet, so I had to wait a few years until I was of legal age to enter. In 1999 I started entering sweepstakes online heavily. I would look at all the sweepstakes I could find on all the different websites. I would spend hours and hours entering in my free time. I didn't win much early on. My first couple decent wins were a socket set, a size large Olympic sweatshirt, and some contact solution. At the time I won the socket set, which was valued at $34, they wanted me to get an affidavit signed by a public notary. I had no idea what that meant at the time. I would dip into sweeping in spurts. In 2009 I won a flip camera in a picture contest and I jumped into video contests. My first big win was a $5,000 prize from Transitions lenses. Looking back now, the video was pretty rough, but it had a good idea at the heart of it, which is why I think it won. I've gone on to win multiple picture contests and video contests. A few highlight wins are: a Mini Cooper Countryman, $10,000 in cash, and a handful of trips.

Q. What win are you most proud of?

A. It actually isn't a win, but I consider it one. I had entered a bug spray video contest and I made a video where I did a "no bugspray dance" where I slapped my arms and legs faster and faster to a bluegrass song. It was very silly. I lost the contest, but the following year the company told me they were going to use my idea of the "no bugspray dance" for their next contest theme. They sent me a check for a few hundred dollars as a thank you for the idea. I thought that was a nice thing for them to do.

Q. What kind of 'sweeping' regimen do you have? (I.e., How do you go about finding out which sweepstakes to enter? How often do you enter? Do you have favorite times to enter? etc).

My 'sweeping' regimen is very hit or miss. I used to go for hours and hours a few years ago (strictly online sweeps) but recently I've pooled my resources into more skill-based contests. I like sweepstakes that make you go to a lot of effort. The more effort and creativity in a contest the better as far as I'm concerned.

Q. Questions from readers (we sent out a newsletter and asked them to submit questions in addition to the above ones, and these were some of them)

a) How do you keep yourself motivated to keep entering?

A. I think this is one of the reasons why I'm successful. I think you need to have an obsessive (and stubborn) quality to win sweepstakes and contests. I think obsessing about certain things, especially negative, or out of your control, is unhealthy and a waste of energy. So, I try to steer my obsessive powers toward things I can control, like sweeps and contests. They are fun and keep my brain occupied. I love brainstorming ideas for my contests. My favorite moment in the course of a contest isn't winning, but that instance where I've come up with the killer idea that I think will win. The idea is always what drives me forward. A great idea can carry me through the frustration of creating the picture or video.

b) When 'exactly' do you enter? (i.e., Do you enter at the beginning, middle or on its last day just a few hours before the sweep is about to close.)

I enter sweepstakes whenever I can, I have no rhyme or reason. I usually do it during a regular day, so no late night or early morning sweeps for me, but I've heard that pays off for some. I'm not very disciplined in my approach. I enter sweepstakes in sprints, not a steady jog. I enter contests in spurts as well. I like to take a little time off every so often to enjoy the fruits of my labors. I have noticed that contests and sweepstakes are seasonal and predictable. Right now it is the middle of summer, so companies are running contests with... wait for it... a summer theme. Mind blowing stuff, huh?

c) What conventions/tradeshows/groups/etc do you take part in to increase your chances of winning?

I go to the sweepstakes conventions, last year in Atlanta, and this year in Salt Lake City. It is nice to talk shop with so many people, especially because my friends don't show any interest in sweeping or contesting. I do have friends that say "Hey! Win me an iPad!" And I ask them what they would like to do to win it, and they just want me to win it for them. I am not in any local group, but I'd really like to form a comedy troupe of sorts that could make videos together. I'm in the central Kentucky area, and far from comedy spots like LA, NY and Chicago, so it is a little tough finding similar minded people.

d) Do you have any recommendations on how to track your wins? (I.e., Excel spreadsheets? Any software, etc?)

I track my wins, losses, and future contests in Google Spreadsheet. It is nice because it is online and I can access it anywhere. I will put "won", "lost", or "did not enter" in the spreadsheet. I realized that when I did not enter a contest I should immediately mark it as lost since my chances were zero. That is when I realized that you lose every contest you don't enter. So it motivated me to enter more. Because you can't win if you don't enter!

e) Any tips on finding 'local' sweepstakes?

This is one of my weakest areas. I'd love to find more local sweepstakes. Especially contests.

Q. What kinds of tools/websites/resources do you use to enter Sweepstakes?

A. I use http://www.online-sweepstakes.com/, http://www.about.com/, and http://www.onlinevideocontests.com/ mainly. I also use "Google Alerts" for specific things I want to win. For example I currently have a Google alert for "backyard makeover" sweepstakes and contests.

Q. What one 'secret' tip that few people know about, could you share with people to help them increase their chances of winning?

A. The magic word is "effort." The more effort a sweepstakes requires, the less people enter. When I see a sweepstakes or contest and think "Yuck, too much work" – I am now obligated to enter it. If a sweeper like myself thinks it is too much work, I just imagine a non-sweeper passing it right by. So, less entries = more chances.

Q. Anything else you think might be interesting to people reading this?

A. I enter primarily skill based contests. I improve with each project, or at least try to improve. I try to parlay my winnings towards the next prize. I reinvest in my equipment and I try to learn as I go. I think it pays to foolishly jump into some of these contests, because you never know what's going to happen.

Interview with Carol McLaughlin

I met Carol at the Michigan Sweepstakes Convention. She was very friendly, very nice and I had quite an enjoyable talk with her. She runs the "This N' That Sweepstakes Club" newsletter, as well is the host of the Pennsylvania convention. She agreed to an interview, and was very gracious to offer her tips and strategies on how you can increase your chances of winning!

Q. Please tell me a bit about yourself. How did you get started entering sweepstakes?

A. I started entering contests casually as a teen around 1968/69 doing radio contests and also watching my mother win radio contests. We were too young to enter so watching Mom was fun. BUT, she was not what I'd call a sweeper in today's terms – just casual here and there. I'd enter a little here and there if I saw something in the newspaper or on a product container. But, I didn't start winning regularly until I subscribed to the Contest Newsletter, which I found in a Publisher's Clearing House magazine promotion. From there I found out that there were other newsletters and subscribed to all of them, getting up to seven sweeps newsletter at one time. Many of them quit publishing and many of them were sold to SweepSheet so my SweepSheet subscription was constantly being extended with the extra issues I had paid for.

Q. What was your first big win that got you 'hooked'? What have you won since then?

A. Thinking back there were loads of small prizes coming my way, but my first "biggest" came around 1997 when I won a fully paid trip for four to Walt Disney World. I believe the sponsor was Target. It was for 4 days and 3 nights, but we extended it to 5 days and 4 nights so that we could take direct flights both ways. They put us up in the Contemporary Hotel so that we could just zip right in and out of the park on the Monorail. It included all meals, all tipping - and we didn't know it, but Disney picked up the bill for the extra day! Needless to say we were all spoiled. Imagine a 10 and 11 year old eating prime rib and lobster tails, drinking cappuccino, to name a few things I remember them eating.

Q. What win are you most proud of?

The win I am most proud of was a call I received one evening late (around 9:30 pm.EST). I thought it was a joke because it was so late in the evening. When I answered the phone the gentleman on the other end asked for me by name. I replied, "Yes, this is Carol." He responded by saying, "Congratulations, you just won the NBC/Strawbridge Home for the Holidays Sweepstakes". He then asked if I remembered entering. I did remember entering, but didn't remember what all of the prize included. He told me that I won airfare for two to anywhere in the continental United States and asked if I knew where I wanted to go. I told him that my son was in the Navy and that I'd like to fly to Texas to see him if the base would allow it. He thought that was just great. Then he said, "Do you know what else you won? -- And then told me that I won a gift certificate to Strawbridge's in the amount of $1,000. I said that the money would come in really great in time for Christmas shopping. Then he said, "And..." I went, "And...?" He replied, "You also won a check in the amount for (I think it was) $450 to go food shopping at the store of my choice." In wrapping up the conversation we talked about my need to contact my son and get security clearance and I told him that I didn't like to fly in the winter months because of ice and snow. He was about to go on vacation (this was around mid-December) so we decided that I would wait and talk to my son and we'd talk again after the 1st of the year. The beginning of January we talked and I told him that I'd like to take the trip around April or May. However, I'd wanted to hold off on airline reservations till the last minute so that I could be sure that my son would not be re-stationed somewhere. He then gave me the surprise of my life... he told me that he had talked to the sponsors and they had all agreed to just send me a check for the total amount of the prize $2,400 so that I could just call and make arrangements whenever I wanted to go to see him.

I booked a trip for my other son and I to go down in the spring and met I my son, daughter-in-law and my little granddaughter who was 9 months old at the time. I hadn't seen them since she was born. It was so exciting! What I did next was what I really enjoyed... I took my daughter-in-law food shopping and spent around $500 filling their refrigerator, freezer, cabinets and even under the kitchen table with food for them, their dog and their cat. I told my son when we got to the house, "I bought the food, now you can carry it all in." Needless to say he was shocked. My daughter-in-law knew she didn't have enough money to pay for all that food, but didn't know what I was up to. Then I also took some more of the money and treated the five of us to a day at Sea World San Antonio which was only ten minutes or so from their house. It was fun watching the baby watch the killer whales and animals.

When I got home I still had some money left. My siblings had planned a trip to Las Vegas to take my niece there for her 21st birthday, so I paid for airfare for myself, my younger son and my boyfriend at the time to go to Vegas. I also paid for the hotel bill out of my own pocket, but left the dinner bill and souvenir shopping, etc. up to the guys. So in closing it was one prize win that I was grateful to NBC and Strawbridge in giving me the opportunity to not only see my son, whom we dearly missed, but to make what I call four wins out of the money!

Q. What kind of 'sweeping' regimen do you have?

A. As much as I'd like to say I have a "magic" routine, I really enter my sweepstakes as I can find the time. Actually, I call it "when the spirit moves me", because I keep up a household, publish a newsletter, attend all kinds of sweepstakes functions, try to stay involved in local activities and spend a lot of time with my fiancé and family.

Q. How do you go about finding out which sweepstakes to

enter?

A. I find out about sweepstakes to enter from all kinds of sources: while food shopping with ads or promotions on food packaging, by using newsletters that list sweepstakes such as http://www.online-sweepstakes.com/, SweepSheet, Sweeping America, http://www.sweepsu.com/, your [SweepersChoice] sweepstakes alerts, emails received from sponsors listing sweepstakes, attending my local sweepstakes club (Philly Cheesestakers) meetings and visiting other clubs in the area on occasion, attending other mini and national sweepstakes conventions, meeting people who attend the mini convention (Northeast Mini Sweepstakes Convention) that I run, which is held normally in October each year. I even have my own family come tell me of sweepstakes they hear and see now that they see I do really win! However, they would rather leave the entering to me.

Q. How often do you enter?

A. I don't enter on a set routine. It's when I have the time and usually while we are watching TV in the evening or during the early morning when the house is quiet. I like to take my Sundays and do my catching up when I know I am falling behind. I'd say that on an average I enter about 200-300 sweepstakes a day about three times a week, and then about 200 mailed sweepstakes a month. Again, these numbers increase depending on the amount of spare time I take out of my days and what is going on at the household. I live alone and until just recently I had the one son living with me, so it was making dinner and cleaning up after him, and then also watching and doing things with the granddaughter who now lives close by.

Q. Do you have favorite times to enter?

A. I don't have any set times to enter, but do like to do it when the rest of the gang is out of the house or they are involved in doing other things. That way I am not interrupted or ignoring them. I do sometimes sit and enter and discuss sweepstakes with my son, granddaughter and fiancé on what we would like to do as far as trips, etc. I do get really excited when I see a good sweepstakes and guess whose ears I end up bending! lolol They all used to think I was crazy, but as the prizes have been coming in more and more and the trips are getting better and better, I have caught them discussing my hobby with their friends. A lot of the stuff in my household has been won over the years!

If I had to pick times... it's usually early in the morning or very late at night. I don't think there is a special time to enter. I think it's all in keeping a positive attitude... I enter and let it go to the Universe and move on to the next sweepstakes... I never fret about not winning a particular sweepstakes or if I have a dry spell. I know there will be something coming around the corner.

Q. Questions from readers (we sent out a newsletter and asked them to submit questions in addition to the above ones, and these were some of them)

a) How do you keep yourself motivated to keep entering?

A. I regularly attend sweepstakes club meetings and events such as the mini and national conventions where we talk about our wins. Getting excited for another person's wins is just as rewarding as winning it yourself. I believe in thinking positive and keeping a positive attitude towards the hobby. I love the element of surprise... I know I will win something... watching the UPS, FedEx or Mailman coming to the door with a package or letter is sooooo exciting... it's like Christmas or Birthday all year long! I also publish the This N' That Sweepstakes Club Newsletter so I get to interact with other sweepers in helping them with their questions about sweepstakes. I list their wins and stories in the newsletter for all to read. Many sweepers don't get a chance to attend meetings or conventions so this helps them keep in the loop so to speak. I just love my hobby!

b) When 'exactly' do you enter? (i.e., Do you enter at the beginning, middle or on its last day just a few hours before the sweep is about to close.)

A. You have to enter throughout the entire time that the sweepstakes is open, using good judgment budget wise, and hope that your energy stays with the entry so that it is picked. I have repeatedly told new sweepers that there is no "magic" to winning. They just have to see the sweepstakes, if they saw it then their energy is already in motion; decide if they want to enter it; if so, send off the entry and let it go. With so many sweepstakes being offered at any given time there is no way that everyone can enter every sweepstakes. So, if they fall upon seeing it - it was meant to be -- enter it if they want the prize! I DO NOT believe in entering "just to win" or "to sell" the prizes-- bad karma to me. And I DO thank my sponsors -- and more importantly, show grace and patience to the sponsors when their prizes or delayed or a problem comes up. By doing so, there are a couple of occasions where I was patient with them fulfilling my prize and I made out better in the long run... take for instance my NBC win...

c) What conventions/tradeshows/groups/etc do you take part in to increase your chances of winning?

A. The Northeast Mini Sweepstakes Convention that I run of course! lolol I also have attended the last nine national sweepstakes conventions, plus two sweepstakes banquets held in other states on a yearly basis. I belong to our local sweepstakers club - the Philly Cheesestakers. Hey, I'll attend anything that has to do with sweepstakes. Several sweepstakes friends have already buddied up with me and we shared trips as travel companions.

d) Do you have any recommendations on how to track your wins? (I.e., Excel spreadsheets? Any software, etc?)

A. I track all of my entries using the tracking system on Online-sweepstakes.com. I have been using them for so long that I found it difficult to try to go to another system. I have, however, recently started using SweepsU.com which also has a great tracking system. There are others out there such as Sweepstakes Tracker run by Dana Noga, which I am familiar with and would also recommend. These tracking systems I recommend for entering online sweepstakes. For my postal entries I just mark the sweepstakes in the printed issue with the date as I enter them and file the issues in a binder. I do keep a steno list with all of my one per person, one per household entries listed by the month they expire. I do keep my win notifications in a separate binder in date order. Looking back through them, especially when you think you are in a dry spell will really let you realize just how lucky you really are.

e) Any tips on finding 'local' sweepstakes?

A. Best thing is to read the newspapers and listen to the radio for their advertisements. Also, belonging to a sweepstakes club helps because it is more than one set of eyes on the lookout for them. Yep, real sweepers are not afraid to share their finds... we enjoy hearing when it's someone whom we know who wins if it is not us.

Q. What kinds of tools/websites/resources do you use to enter Sweepstakes?

A. I use Roborform or Chrome's autofill to speed up entering my sweepstakes. Websites: Online-sweepstakes.com, SweepsU.com, Sweeping America and SweepSheet. Then if I see anything in my emails or on Facebook I'll also enter.

Q. What one 'secret' tip that few people know about, could you share with people to help them increase their chances of winning?

The only tip of any value --- "READ THE DIRECTIONS"! I have held and run promotions and almost every single time there are about 20% of the entries that are disqualified for not following the rules. Not giving the information that was requested; missing the deadline dates; entering too many times to name a few. There is no real "Secret" to winning. It just has to be done correctly.

Q. Anything else you think might be interesting to people reading this?

The only thing I can say is to make a budget for spending on issues and postage, etc. and stick to it; try to join a club and/or attend sweepstakes conventions; definitely be sure you check your entries to be sure you did it right before sending it off... even seasoned sweepers for many years still make mistakes! Even me on occasion! And make it fun... if it feels like a job... then give it a break... it should be fun while you are entering and waiting for that win. Subscribe to the various newsletters!

Q. Please talk about the Northeast Mini Convention/Pennsylvania convention. What is it about, how long it has been going, why people should come, how they can sign up, and more.

The Northeast Mini Sweepstakes Convention was started as what was to be a few women from our club getting together for a weekend away pajama party in which we'd bring some gifts and raffle prizes and talk sweeping. We decided to have it somewhere out of town. Then some of us knew other sweepers that belonged to other clubs and they asked if they could join us... sure... then they wanted to bring spouses along... we dropped the PJ party part... and looked for something more central to Pennsylvania. Then sweepers from out of state asked if they could join... sure... so we stepped it up to instead of having a one night event to changing it to make it mirror what the National Sweepstakes Convention does - only ours would be over a weekend and in no way compete against National. It was developed to promote my sweepstakes business at the time "Ann-tics by Carol Sweepstakes Supplies" and then later to introduce and still to this day to promote my newsletter "This N' That Sweepstakes Club Newsletter". This I found would give me a chance to meet my subscribers face-to-face and also to introduce myself to new subscribers.

I always hold it in October, but not every single year (my family schedule takes priority). This year will be my sixth one. It is held just outside of Hershey, PA in a town called Grantville. The convention opens for early registration on Friday afternoon, and then the main kick-off is Friday evening with a Meet & Greet.

Then we have speakers and a session with prizes all day Saturday, and a Banquet with more prizes on Saturday evening. We have a session Sunday morning and break by noon. It is geared for attendees only... family members taking the trip with the attendees are not permitted in the convention area or to participate in any of the activities. So, we suggest that they either register as an attendee, have something else to keep them busy all weekend long, or not join them on the trip. It is a very compact schedule all weekend because of where the hotel lies. In previous years there was nothing around to do, they have recently built and opened a casino within a few minutes of the hotel. It is designed to give attendees a taste of what goes on at a National Convention only on a much smaller prize scale and cost scale. All prizes are donated by attendees and friends/vendors of sweepers. We do not carry any corporate sponsors for this event and it is registered as a private party. With that being said all registration forms must be requested by emailing our committee at our email address with their name and address for our files.

We DO NOT allow any walk-ins, stop-ins or drop-ins at our convention. Anyone showing up at the door without being pre-registered does get turned away. There are positively no exceptions. The hotel is under strict orders that there is to be no news media dropping in to cover any of this event. It is a private affair and many of our attendees do not want to be filmed.

Right now we are very close to selling out and it is on a first come, first paid basis. We cannot, to be fair to everyone, "hold" spots for anyone.

Again, it is geared more towards those coming from the USA
because most of our prizes are sweepstakes and postal mail
related, i.e., stamps, envelopes, postcards, gift baskets of
sweeping supplies, etc. Anyone is welcome to come, but we
don't want to mislead anyone as to what we do.

6. Sweepstakes Frequently Asked Questions

Here is a list of common questions that I have heard concerning sweepstakes. And here are those answers.

Q. "I haven't won anything yet! How come?"

A. Because if you are selected as a winner, it usually takes 60-90 days from the first time you enter a sweepstakes.

While I have found most people understand how sweepstakes work, periodically I get e-mails from people who have literally 'just' entered once or twice, one or two days ago – and wonder why they haven't won thousands of dollars of prizes yet...

a) Most sweepstakes run for <u>at least</u> 30 days. Many run for 60-90 days. After that, it may take them another 30 days to get necessary affidavits (for publicity purposes – basically getting permission from you to republish your name). So it is quite possible, that <u>if</u> you were selected as a winner, that it could take <u>up to</u> 4 months before you even <u>see</u> a prize. Not that it *would* take that long, but it *could*.

b) Second, it's important to remember that there is no guarantee that you will win a prize. While it's true that the more you enter – the more likely you are to win – it could be possible that you just hit a cold streak. But sweepstakes **IS** a numbers game – and the more you enter – the more likely you are to win. And paraphrasing one man that has won over TWO

HUNDRED vacations in his lifetime said – *when the going gets tough, the tough get going!* He enters <u>more</u> when he's on a 'cold' streak than when he's winning... So keep that in mind if it seems you haven't won anything for a little while...

Q. "I haven't received my prize yet? Why not?"

A. Sometimes people get very worried. Sometimes sponsors make mistakes, and sometimes technology does not work. So just because you have not yet received a prize, does not mean that it is a fake sweepstakes. Chances are, there is some kind of miscommunication or error. By doing the following, you can help ensure that you receive your prize.

a) <u>Try sending from a different e-mail address.</u> Sometimes, for whatever reason, e-mails get lost in spam filters. Or, yours may not just get sent. So if a sponsor was expecting an affidavit from you and you never got a confirmation e-mail from them, then it is quite possible that they never saw your e-mail. I always recommend adding a note in your e-mail saying something along the lines of "please confirm receipt of this e-mail". If they do not do that within 1-2 days, then it is possible they never received it -- and you can try sending from another e-mail address.

B) <u>It may be at customs if it has to cross the border.</u> Some sweepstakes run in both Canada and the US. If the company has to send the prize across the border -- then it is possible that it might be at the border, and they want you to pay duty on it. If this is the case, you can contact the company to see if they can take care of that. Or, you could always drive to the border yourself, and pick it up.

c) Be patient. While it would be wonderful if you received a prize as soon as you have heard that you won it, that rarely happens. In fact, sometimes companies may take up to 3 to 4 weeks just to send the prize out. That is because they are working with sponsors who then have to go through the proper channels in their company, to get everything sent out. And then of course, when it is sent through the mail, it can take another 1-2 weeks. If, however, you have not received anything six weeks after you have been notified that you were a winner, then you can follow up with the company to see what the status of your prize is.

Q. "What do I do if I don't get my prize?"

A. There are a number of steps you can take to help ensure you receive your prize.

Step One: Don't panic. Relax. If you panic, then you will get very stressed, and this can defeat the purpose of having fun entering sweepstakes.

Step Two: Take a step by step action plan.

You need to remember that behind every sweepstakes, is a person running that sweepstakes. Sometimes they are happy, sometimes they are sad, sometimes they get very busy, and sometimes they forget. People make mistakes. And sometimes companies get acquired, sold, and so forth – so the person running the original sweepstakes is no longer with the company. So subsequently, sometimes, it is possible that you may not (initially) get your prize. It is not because of malicious intent, it is usually just because 'stuff happens'. (I'd use a different word, but I'd like to keep this book family friendly! ☺)

So this is what you can do.

a) <u>Take a deep breath.</u> No point in getting worked up. And WAIT six weeks before doing any of this. Sometimes prizes take a long time to ship, and be delivered. Last thing you want to do is to get upset, only to find you receive the prize the next day.

b) If you have not received the prize after <u>4-6 weeks</u>, then e-mail <u>once or twice</u> over the next week. Do <u>NOT</u> e-mail more than once a day. While the prize is important to you – many individuals within companies have many things on their plate. If you start incessantly e-mailing them, it can come across very annoying, and you may end up not getting the prize at all. You've probably hear the expression 'Patience is a virtue' as a child, and in this case it is. You can be consistent, and persistent when e-mailing – but be patient. Give the sponsor time to respond.

c) If after about 1-2 weeks, and e-mailing, you still don't hear a response, pick up the phone. Try to find someone to talk to in the company about the promotion.

d) If you can't find anyone – look for the sponsor, or the 'main' company sponsoring the sweepstakes. There was a large company called Promotions.com that was recently acquired by another company called EPrize. As luck would have it, many people didn't get their prizes during the transition, because people were being moved around. So some individuals contacted the companies sponsoring the sweepstakes, and gently asked them if they could look into it. And then they received their prizes.

e) If you STILL don't get the prize after following all the above steps, move on. Sometimes – "stuff happens". And you might not get a prize. There are tens of thousands of sweepstakes out there on a regular, monthly basis – and your time & energy is better spent entering new sweepstakes, than getting worked up about a single prize. Sometimes, "stuff happens" – and you need to move on.

Step Three: SMILE! Providing you followed all of the above steps, most likely your prize is on its way. So relax, take a deep breath – and start entering new sweepstakes! And when your prize arrives at the door, get excited, and **make sure you thank the sponsor**!

Q. If a sweepstakes says one entry per person, does this mean that I can enter for my wife / husband / son / daughter from the same computer/IP address?

A. Generally speaking, the answer is yes.
Unless the sweepstakes explicitly says that it's one per

household (which also generally means one person per physical mailing address), then it is usually okay.

You do need to remember though, that every organization has its own rules. Some companies may strictly monitor if more than one entry is made, and automatically delete the rest. Other companies may prevent you from entering more than once, by showing a message saying "You've already entered for today". While finally, other companies find it's too much work to sort through legitimate and non-legitimate entries, and will just pick someone at random. Sweepstakes are run by people, and while computers might make running sweepstakes easier, behind the computer is a real person.

Q. Is it okay if I use a form filler, or a software tool that helps me enter sweepstakes?

A. This question has been debated over and over in various sweepstakes forms, but the short answer is that in most cases, yes.

The purpose of a company running a promotion is to get marketing exposure, brand recognition, word-of-mouth advertising, and so forth. If you actually visit their website, know the promotion that you are entering, and know what prizes you have a chance of winning -- then generally speaking the companies don't mind if you use form filling software. That is because they are getting the brand recognition/advertising for hosting the sweepstakes that they desire.

You have to remember that behind each sweepstakes, is a real person managing the promotion. If they see that people are indeed engaging with their brand, then they are usually quite happy.

You also need to remember that each sweepstakes is different. While most don't mind, some might. It is always important to read the rules. That being said, I have personally read numerous winning stories (literally hundreds of them) in which someone won a prize, and admitted to using a form filler to help speed up the process.

Q. How do I prevent disqualification?

A. You need to remember that it is up to the individual sponsor to decide, but as a general rule of thumb if you do any of the following, it could possibly get you disqualified.

(a) **Don't enter more than you are allowed.** If the sweepstakes says you're allowed to enter once per day, and you enter 10 times per day, most likely all of your additional entries will be disqualified. In some cases all of your entries may be disqualified, because the company thinks you are trying to abuse the system.

(b) **Don't Abuse unlimited entries.** There are some companies that still allow you to have unlimited entries. That means, you could sit in front of the computer all day, and keep on entering the sweepstakes. But even though it says "unlimited", in many cases it's not really "unlimited". This is because companies are smart enough to know when it's a person doing it as opposed to a computer script. Realistically, in a day, a real person might at most enter 100 times for an "unlimited" sweepstakes. If, however, there are 100,000 entries in 10 minutes, the company will deduce that their system is being abused, and most likely disqualify that individual.

(c) **Don't have someone else enter for you (i.e., entering <u>not</u> from your own computer).** If you do not actually enter the sweepstakes from your own computer, then you may be disqualified. Simply because, if a company sees hundreds of different entries for hundreds of different individuals coming from the same IP address (a.k.a. the same computer), then they will most likely disqualify those entries. This is simply because the person being entered probably has no idea of what they are being entered for.

(d) **Don't enter for multiple people "in excess".** While most companies will let you enter for, say, a son or daughter, a husband or wife, and so forth -- if you start entering for 20 or 30 different people, chances are they will disqualify those entries, and yours as well. This is simply because, there are some people who will indeed make up fake names and fake addresses just to try and win a prize. Sponsors are smart enough to recognize this, and if it appears it is being abused, pretty much all entries from the same computer will be disqualified.

7. Tools and Resources

This section is devoted to discussing various online tools and resources, that you can use to help increase your chances of finding and winning more sweepstakes. This list is constantly changing however. As a matter of fact – as I was writing this book – certain websites/references that I used for the last couple years no longer exist. At the same time, new resources only a few months old were appearing. Sometimes a search engine, or group of fellow sweepers can be your best friend. And of course, this book as well!

Software Tools

SweepersChoice

SweepersChoice is an excellent application for sweepers. It is a sweepstakes organizer, and form filling application designed exclusively for people who like to enter sweepstakes.

SweepersChoice has 'one-click' sweepstakes. This is a list of sweepstakes from various companies around the USA. You simply enter your personal information once (that is, where any prizes you win should be sent) -- and then click a button to enter the sweepstakes. This list is updated on a very regular basis (usually once a week, sometimes even several times a week) – so it is always up to date. You can usually get anywhere from 300-450 sweepstakes on any given day. And then, you can get entered into those sweepstakes within 15-20 minutes, as opposed to four or five hours. Done daily – this can literally save you 40-50 hours/month that you can use for other things, such as enjoying the prizes you do win, or spending it with family.

Complete details can be found here:
http://www.sweeperschoice.com/

SweepersChoice – CAPTCHA Sweepstakes

As of 2013, SweepersChoice now can process 'CAPTCHA' style sweepstakes. CAPTCHAs are those hard to read words/images. SweepersChoice can now help you enter those sweepstakes with the click of a button. There are three levels of CAPTCHA support. One supports an additional 25-75 daily CAPTCHA sweepstakes, the second level supports 75-225 daily CAPTCHA sweepstakes. And, we just recently added a 3rd level of support that supports up to 400 daily CAPTCHA sweepstakes.

If you've entered a CAPTCHA before, you know how hard it can be to read, and what a strain on your eyes it is. SweepersChoice makes this easy for you, so you don't have to worry about it. Instead of taking 2-3 hours entering 100 CAPTCHA sweepstakes, you can do this in minutes.

CAPTCHA support is available, and only available, as an add-on to existing SweepersChoice PREMIUM members.

SweepersChoice – MILLIONAIRES Club

The SweepersChoice MILLIONAIRES Club is an _exclusive_ club limited to 100 people, maximum.

Some people like to win only big prizes, such as cars, cash prizes, electronics, vacation packages, and so forth. The MILLIONAIRES club focuses exclusively on these types of sweepstakes. Club members are guaranteed access to at least 100 additional sweepstakes per month. The combined total prize pool of these sweepstakes in a single month is one million dollars, or more. And every single sweepstake usually has at least one 'major' prize. _[EDIT: After the first couple months, we were really excited to find out that a few people were already starting to have big wins! A few users told us about a $600 cosmetics package, $2,400 NASCAR Vacation, and a $7,000 vacation to London, England!]_

Since the bigger prize sweepstakes tend to be harder to enter (CAPTCHAs, memberships, surveys, multi-form sweepstakes, and so forth) – it is a lot of work to add these sweepstakes to the software. However, since it is an exclusive club, SweepersChoice MILLIONAIRES club members can process these sweepstakes in minutes, not hours.

Sweepstakes include prizes such as sports cars, luxury cruises or vacations, high-end electronics, or large cash prizes. This club is limited exclusively to 100 people. Once it has been filled up, no one can join unless someone else leaves. You may get more

details of the millionaires club by going to this URL:
http://www.sweeperschoice.com/products-millionaires.php

Roboform

For sweepers who don't mind spending hours a day searching
for sweepstakes, and finding the ones they want to enter,
Roboform can be a very useful tool.

Roboform is a form filler that facilitates filling in forms when
entering sweepstakes. While it cannot find the sweepstakes for
you, it can save you some time when you fill in the form.
Complete details can be found here:

http://www.roboform.com/

Other Form Fillers

There are a number of other form fillers on the market,
everything from free, to free/paid, to paid. The thing to note is
that they all vary in how 'good' they are at processing forms.
Many can only fill in 'basic' types of website forms, but as soon
as you get anything semi-complicated, they don't work.

That being said, here are other form fillers you can use:

Google Autofill/Safari Auto-Fill –
Good for basic forms, but fails on anything more complicated

LastPass - http://www.lastpass.com/
Form filler similar to Roboform, except a competing product.
Designed to work on PCs.

1Password - http://www.agilebits.com/onepassword
Password form/filler designed to work on a Macintosh system.

Sweepstakes Tracker

Sweepstakes Tracker is more of a software tool designed to help
you organize your sweepstakes. It is designed to be used in
conjunction with a form filler, but does have some form filling
capabilities. It does have some useful add-ons, such as the
ability to track costs associated with sweeping (as well as your
prize winnings). Complete details can be found here:

http://www.sweepstakestracker.com/

Spybot – Search And Destroy!

I personally find this an incredibly useful tool. While entering
sweepstakes can be a lot of fun, unfortunately from time to
time some unscrupulous characters will try to install software
(spyware) on your computer, without your knowledge.

Generally speaking, they tend to be things like search toolbars,
affiliate toolbars, and so forth. What happens is that your
computer becomes really slow, and sometimes it can become
difficult to enter sweepstakes.

This software tool is very useful at removing those unwanted programs. After running it once or twice, you can sometimes find that entering sweepstakes speeds up by 200% to 300%. I have personally installed this tool on a friend's computer who found that their computer was running very slowly. And I saw their computer speed up significantly after running this tool. So, if you suspect that you may have accidentally installed something you didn't mean to, then it might be worth trying out this software tool.

http://www.safer-networking.org/

Sticky Notes

There are a number of software applications that allow you to easily create sticky notes. They are just like the real Post-It notes, except they are on your computer desktop. Sometimes people find that it helps them remember certain sweepstakes that they want to enter, especially if they are daily sweepstakes. Since there are so many of these types of software applications, I recommend going into a search engine, and typing in "sticky notes software", and then deciding which software application best suits your needs.

'Cleaning' Your Computer

While not technically a 3rd party software application, I recommend doing this if you are going to be entering sweepstakes on a regular basis. Ideally, every 3-6 months you

should 'clean' your computer, just like you would do an oil
change for your car.

By 'cleaning', I mean doing a complete erase & re-install of all
your software on your computer. Of course – backup any
important files to a USB drive first. Then, format & re-install
your computer.

This is simply because, over time – you will most likely
inadvertently install spyware, or other rogue software on your
computer systems. While 'anti-spyware' and 'anti-virus'
software is 'good', some spyware, viruses, trojans and so forth
are better. The result is that you will tend to notice your
computer running a lot slower.

The easiest & quickest remedy is to simply re-install your
computer from scratch. It will format your computer, and then
set it up as if you just purchased it from the computer store.

And then you will notice it running a lot faster, and you can
enjoy sweeping again!

Other Software Tools

There are a number of the other software tools available, but I
have chosen not to include them because they are not
maintained any longer. However, doing a search in any search
engine for terms such as "enter sweepstakes online" or "enter
sweepstakes automatically" can help you find them. Then, you

can evaluate for yourself whether or not they can help you.

A few important points to consider when evaluating software tools are as follows:

a) Do you enter from your own computer?
b) Do you get to choose the sweepstakes to enter?
c) Do they have an active community ? (i.e. regular users in website forums?)
d) Can it help save you time?
e) Does it help you become more efficient at entering sweepstakes?

If you can answer yes to one or more of the above questions, then it may be worthwhile trying out the software or service.

Website resources

The list of websites, tools and resources for finding and entering sweepstakes is constantly changing. However, the following websites have been around for a while, and are most likely to be around for a while longer. So you may check these resources for more information about sweepstakes. Everything here is organized alphabetically.

Sweepstakes Directories/Finding Sweepstakes:

About.Com Sweepstakes - http://contests.about.com/od/sweepstakeslistings/a/newsweepstakes.htm

Big Sweeps - http://www.bigsweeps.com/

Cashnet Sweeps - http://www.cashnetsweeps.com/

Enter Online Sweeps - http://www.enteronlinesweeps.com/

FindPrizesNow.com - http://www.findprizesnow.com/

Infinite Sweeps - http://www.infinitesweeps.com/

Online-Sweepstakes - http://www.online-sweepstakes.com/

Our Instant Win - http://www.ourinstantwin.com/

Snazzy Wins - http://snazzywin.com/instants.html

Sweeps Advantage - http://www.sweepsadvantage.com/

Sweepstakes Bananas - http://sweepstakesbananas.com/

Sweepstakes Depot - http://www.sweepstakesdepot.com/

Sweepstakes Lovers- http://www.sweepstakeslovers.com/

SweepstakesMax – http://www.sweepstakesmax.com/

Sweepstakes Fanatics - http://www.sweepstakesfanatics.com/

Sweepstakes Today - http://www.sweepstakestoday.com/

Sweeties Sweeps - http://www.sweetiessweeps.com/

Contest Directories/Finding Contests:

Many of these sites are geared towards entering Canadian sweepstakes (aka 'contests'). Some however, do have USA 'skill-based' contests.

Canada Contests - http://www.cancontests.com/

Canada Sweepstakes - http://www.canadasweepstakes.ca/

Contest Blogger - http://www.contestblogger.com/

Contest Girl - http://contestgirl.com/

Contest Heat - http://www.contestheat.com/

Contest Hound - http://www.contesthound.ca/

Contest Life - http://www.contestlife.com/

Contest Listing - http://www.contestlisting.com/

Contest Mob – http://www.contestmob.com/

Contest Queen - http://www.contestqueen.com/

Fat Wallet -
http://www.fatwallet.com/forums/contests-and-sweepstakes/

I Win Contests - http://www.iwincontests.com/

Lucky Day Contests - http://www.luckydaycontests.com/

RedFlagDeals – http://www.redflagdeals.com/

Website Forums:

Online-Sweepstakes – http://forums.online-sweepstakes.com/

Sweeps Advantage –
http://www.sweepsadvantage.com/forum/forum.php

SweepersChoice - http://www.sweeperschoiceforums.com/

SweepsU – http://www.sweepsu.com/

Other (Newsletters):

Best Sweepstakes - http://www.bestsweepstakes.com/

SweepSheet – http://www.sweepsheet.com/

Sweeping America - http://www.sweepingamerica.com/

SweepersChoice - http://www.sweeperschoice.com/

Sweeties Sweeps - http://www.sweetiessweeps.com/

Giveaway Websites:

EZWinGame - http://www.ezwingame.com/

ILoveFreeThings - http://ilovefreethings.com/

GadgetGobble - http://gadgetgobble.com/

JustFreeStuff – http://www.justfreestuff.com/

Royal Draw - http://www.royaldraw.com/

WannaWin.ca - http://www.wannawin.ca/

WinJunkie.com - http://www.winjunkie.com/

Couponing Websites

These are websites where you can get things for free, 'sometimes'! But, at the very least, you should be able to save a lot on your regular purchases!

Retail Me Not - http://www.retailmenot.com/

Coupons.com - http://www.coupons.com/

Coupon Sherpa - http://www.couponsherpa.com/

Go Sampling - http://www.gosampling.com/free-coupons/

Royal Coupon - http://www.royalcoupon.com/

Groupon – http://www.groupon.com/

UPC Code Databases

UPC Machine - http://www.upcmachine.com/

UPC Database - http://www.upcdatabase.com/

UPC Database (.org) - http://upcdatabase.org/search

8. The Good, The Bad, and The Ugly

Entering sweepstakes can be a fun and exhilarating hobby. It can be even more fun when you win amazing prizes! However, sometimes there is a 'dark side' to sweepstakes that you should be aware of. But, as with most things in life, if you take the proper precautions, then you should be perfectly safe and can really enjoy entering sweepstakes. This chapter will be divided into several sections that will help to make you aware of certain situations, and how to protect yourself.

Hidden Sweepstakes Costs

If you win a sweepstakes, there may be hidden sweepstakes costs you don't know about.

If you are based in the USA, which you most likely are if you're reading this book, then you do need to pay taxes on your sweepstakes winnings. If the prize value is under $600, then generally speaking the onus is up to you to record your winnings and pay taxes on those. However, if you win a prize worth more than $600, you will most likely be issued a 1099 form by the company sponsoring the sweepstakes. Usually your winnings would be listed under 'other income' when you file your taxes. Of course, consulting a professional accountant is always a good idea to ensure that everything is done correctly.

ASIDE: Second, if you happen to receive a prize from across the border, whether you are in US or Canada, you may need to pay duty for the prize. Many larger sponsors do take care of this, so you don't have to worry about paying duties. But, if you were expecting a prize, and have not received it for a long time (meaning a couple months after the sponsor said it was sent off), it might be stuck at the border, and so you should look there.

Three "good" notes about the 'hidden' costs.

Number One: When calculating the amount of tax you pay on the prize, you use the fair market value of your prize. So this means if a sponsor said the prize was worth X number of dollars, but in reality you could get the same prize at a cheaper price if you purchased it at a store -- then you would use that fair market value. Just be sure to keep documentation of where you obtained that value, such as receipts, store flyers, and so forth.

Number Two: Second, for larger prizes -- more and more sponsors are recognizing that potential prize winners might find the tax burden a bit daunting. So, more and more sponsors are including cash prizes as part of the prize package to help offset any potential taxes owing. For example, I recently saw a sweepstakes that was advertising the grand prize as being a $60,000 vehicle. However, they were actually including $10,000 cash as part of that price package, explicitly for the purpose of offsetting taxes. So the entire grand prize value was $70,000.

Number Three: If you win a significant amount of prizes, you may be able to deduct the cost of tools used to help you win those prizes. It may be minor, but deductions may include the following: envelopes, stamps, sweepstakes software (form filling software, sweepstakes organizers, sweepstakes spreadsheets, etc, etc), and so forth. <u>Of course, consult with a tax accountant or tax attorney to confirm what you are able to deduct</u>. I am not a tax lawyer. Your eligible deductions may vary from nothing, to all of the above, including depending on your current income level. So I recommend consulting with the appropriate individuals, because you could save a lot!

Fake Sweepstakes – How to Spot Them, and Avoid Entering Them

Sweepstaking can be a lot of fun! The friends you make, the new exciting companies you find out about makes it an exciting hobby! And, one thing that is especially fun, is when you win! :)

However -- unfortunately, some other people try to take advantage of good natured sweepstaking, and try to spoil it for other people. They might use your personal information to try and 'bombard' you with products & services with no real intention of ever awarding a sweepstakes. Other websites may try to get you to download a "search toolbar", because then they get money every time you do a search. The only problem is, it tends to slow down your computer system. And finally, more sinister people might try to asking for a credit card number, which should be a <u>big red flag</u>. For any sweepstakes you enter, you should not have to pay. So, it is important to be able to spot a fake sweepstakes!

Of course, at any time you can go to the list of Sweepstakes that are compiled on a regular basis FindPrizesNow.com website: http://www.findprizesnow.com/

Measures are taken to ensure that only legitimate sweepstakes get listed in here.

Following is a list of potential things to look for when spotting a fake sweepstakes

- **Non-stop surveys are not sweepstakes!** There are some people that try to get you to enter non-stop 'surveys' when entering sweepstakes. While there are legitimate sweepstakes that will ask you to fill in a quick survey (I've seen many automobile ones like Ford do that), if you find yourself in an endless barrage of surveys, then stop. It's most likely not legit. Usually these non-stop survey type questionnaires either sell your information to third parties, or try and get you to buy something right on the spot.

- **Strange Looking Domain Name!** - Most 'legitimate' sweepstakes will either be hosted on a .com extension, the actual 'company' sponsoring the sweepstakes (in which case you can find more info about the company), or a domain containing the name of the brand. (I.e., 'tidedetergentsweepstakes.com' would most likely be legitimate, while 'windetegergent.biz' most likely is not). If it looks fishy (i.e., a ".biz" extension), has a bunch of dashes (i.e., 'super-duper-sweepstakes.com'), or is a very 'generic' name (i.e., "win-a-car.com" versus "wina2013fordmustang.com"), then chances are it is not legit.

- **Web Page Design Too Poor!** - Most companies that run sweepstakes take the time to make sure it looks semi-professional, if not really well done. If it is a poor design, then either it is being run by a single individual. (They don't have the time/money to put together something that looks good), -- OR -- it is just a fake design.

- **Page Design Too Slick!** - On the flip side -- if the page design looks "too" slick – or "too" polished -- then it may also be a 'fake' sweepstakes. Some people (not all) -- called 'Internet Marketers' -- will try to use the psychology of persuasion to try and get you to 'sign up now!'. It may also be for something called a 'CPA' offer - which means 'Cost Per Aquisition', i.e., the person gets 'paid' for every e-mail address they collect, with no real intention of ever offering a sweepstakes. While some CPA offers are legit, i.e., they really do offer a sweepstakes as well, many are not. So if the page design looks "too" slick, then it may also be a fake site.

- **No 'official' rules listed!** - Many 'fly-by-night' operations will forget to list official rules. That's because they really don't care, or simply forget, or have no intention of offering a sweepstakes. If you can't find the rules listed anywhere, then it may be a fake sweepstakes.

-   **"Free" is listed in the domain name.** Ironically -- if it has 'free' listed in the domain, then chances are it's not really free. Those types of sites will try to get you to part with your credit card information before you ever receive anything. One 'popular' variant that is going around nowadays is anything that has 'free ringtones' or 'free iPad', or something along those lines in the domain. Generally speaking, those sites will never award you anything. It is just something called a 'CPA' offer, and has a real hard sell to get you to buy products.

-   **Check the domain registrar.** While this is a little more 'techie', you can check the domain by doing something called a 'WHOIS' search. If the domain information is hidden (i.e., registered via a hidden GoDaddy private registration/domainsbyproxy), or was registered within the last two weeks, then it may be a fake sweepstakes website as well.

If you pay attention to the above tips, then you can help protect yourself against giving information to people who really do not need it.

Two BIG Criteria to Find Legitimate Sweepstakes

There are a few things that EVERY 'legitimate' sweepstakes should have. If it doesn't, then it may be fake.

1. **No-cost entry method required.** There should be a way for you to enter a sweepstakes without paying anything. While some companies do have "paid methods", i.e. purchasing a product or service and entering a product code to get an entry -- they also need to have a no-cost way of entering. Some sweepstakes will have "free codes" you can use listed in the rules. Others will require that you send a mailing envelope to get a free entry self-addressed stamped envelope ("SASE").

2. **They should have official rules.** The rules should outline items such as who may enter, what the timeframe of the promotion is, the types of prizes being offered and their respective value, and so forth. Other items may include skill testing questions (if it is in Canada), and affidavit forms . If a sweepstakes does not have rules, then chances are it is not legitimate.

Getting Rid of Unwanted ('Excessive') Solicitations

Hopefully you're aware, that of course companies that offer sweepstakes will give you special offers from time to time. This is because they're hoping to get good publicity for the prizes they are giving away. Their hope is that their long-term sales will be greater than the prize amount that they gave away. And from time to time, they may follow up with you by phone, or e-mail, to see if you want to purchase their product or service.

This is fine, because you are giving them permission to follow up with you. And, if you're not interested in the product or service, simply let them know -- and most times the companies will be very polite, and thank you for your time, and take you off their list.

However, unfortunately -- there are some companies or individuals that try to abuse this trust. They may try and sell you their product or service, and even though you tell them you don't want it, they persist. This might be in the form of "constant" phone calls, selling you "vacation packages" at great discount, or something along those lines.

If this happens, you can do one or all of the following.

1. **Block their phone number.** Most phone services nowadays allow you to easily block incoming phone calls. You can choose a specific phone number, and request that any calls coming from that number are blocked.

2. **Tell them you are recording the conversation, record it, then play it back.** If it is a company that is constantly calling you and trying to abuse your trust, then this may be an effective tool. Simply because if they are calling you five or six times a day, then it is pretty obvious they're abusing your trust and in many cases further

action could be taken.

How to Protect Yourself from Spam, & Scams

If you are not already a serious sweepstaker (aka 'sweeper'), there are some steps you can take to protect your personal information.

1.**Use an e-mail exclusively devoted for sweepstakes.** While personally I do think you should read sponsors newsletters, because that is one way of supporting them, sometimes it gets to be a bit much. Especially when some send an e-mail every day, or you enter hundreds of sweepstakes. I personally have an e-mail account with over 10,000 e-mail messages. (I still look at many of those messages though!)

2. **Include a middle initial when entering sweepstakes.** Most people just use their first and last name for every type of correspondence and sweepstakes entry. However, if you include a 'different' middle initial say when entering a certain type of sweepstakes, and then start getting a bunch of 'spam' with a specific initial, then you can then identify the source, & get it to stop. (Just contact the person sending out the spam and ask them to stop).

3. **Get a phone number specifically devoted to 'sweepstakes'.** You can get a phone number as 'cheap' as $5/month from online 'phone' answering services. If you enter a lot of sweepstakes, you can use one of these to take your messages.

On the 'off' chance some shady organization tries to abuse your trust – you can get a new phone number easily.

A few different ways of doing this:

a) Google Voice (http://voice.google.com/) – While you may have to pay in the future, at least for the time being you can sign up for a 'Google Voice' account, which will give you a real phone number that you can use exclusively for sweepstakes.

b) Skype Phone Number (http://www.skype.com/) – Skype also offers you the ability to get a phone number very inexpensively. I personally find the Skype service a bit easier to use, so I would recommend that over the Google Voice.

Making sure your Address is Correct - Address Verification

I thought this one was worth mentioning. More and more sweepstakes seem to be using 'address verification', through 3rd party services like http://www.qas.com/ .

What this means is that, if you do not have your address "EXACTLY" the way they have it in their database, your entry will not get submitted. So if for example, you live on "some street NORTH", but forget to put in the 'north', it won't submit. Or, if you live in an apartment building, and don't include the 'unit' number, it won't submit. Or, if it is a P.O. box, and don't have the correct address 'format', i.e., unit #1000, 111 street address, or 1000-111 street address, it won't submit.

So doublecheck to make sure your mailing address is 100% correct to ensure maximum chances at winning.

Plus – as an aside – if you WIN a prize, wouldn't you want to receive it? ☺ So always doublecheck to make sure that your address is correct!

Dealing with "Cheating" (If it Happens)

It actually is pretty hard nowadays to "cheat" when entering sweepstakes, because of all the technology readily available to prevent it. However, a certain type of sweepstakes called 'voting sweepstakes' are still susceptible to cheating.

When the stakes get high – when a company is offering a major prize, like a car or big vacation – other people may get jealous and accuse someone of "cheating". Unfortunately, sometimes people take this too seriously, and forget that sweepstakes are supposed to be fun. In many cases, if someone accuses someone else of "cheating", it is just a case of sour grapes. However, cheating can still happen.

To be clear though, if you enter every day, and the sponsor allows that – it is NOT cheating. That is legitimate. If you promote the sweepstakes to get bonus entries, that is NOT cheating. That is legitimate. It is perfectly legitimate to enter according to allowed frequencies, to enter according to the rules to get bonus entries, and so forth. Using tools to help you organize and enter sweepstakes is NOT cheating. Getting REAL friends to vote for you is NOT cheating.

Accusing someone else of "cheating" when they are not, can sour the promotion and make the sponsor not want to offer prizes again in the future. And, I'm assuming you want to get as many chances as possible to win cool prizes! So, that being said, you should _never_ accuse someone of cheating out of jealousy or envy. This is also because it could come back on you if you incorrectly accused someone, and your entries could be disqualified as well, simply because of a false accusation.

"Cheating" is usually when you circumvent the rules to give yourself an unfair advantage that most other people would not have access to. Cheating is:

- **When you hack into the sponsor's database, and change the results.** Not many people can do this, so it's probably something you don't need to worry about. However, if you did notice some type of exploit, i.e. if you refresh the page or typed in a certain URL and noticed you got entries you aren't supposed to, that could be considered cheating. If anything you should let the sponsor know about it, to ensure that the contest or sweepstakes is run fairly. (In fact, some companies will actually offer you a 'bonus' prize right up front, for being so honorable and honest – and saving them a lot of potential problems!)

- **You create fake accounts or profiles (i.e., Facebook, Twitter accounts, extra e-mail addresses, etc.) to give yourself extra entries.** This, in most instances, would be considered "cheating". While it is true that other people can do exactly the same thing, it tends to run contrary to the spirit of a promotion. (Fake profiles tend to be easy to spot. They either have (a) variations of the person's name (i.e., dave, david, davido, etc), identical birthdays, same set of 'exact' mutual friends, or the "friends" are all promoting the exact same person). The reason this would be considered cheating is because someone can greatly influence the odds of the promotion. (Entering two times would not normally be considered cheating. But if you entered say 2000 times, when "regular" people only once, that could be considered cheating.)

- **"Insider" prizing.** Pretty obvious. If you know someone within the company, and have them choose your name to send your prize, that is cheating. It's also part of the reason why most companies say that employees or family members of employees are not eligible to participate. If you notice anything like this, you might notify the sponsor in private, so that they can fix this and help to make the promotion fun for everyone.

If you notice one of the above three things happening, then you should politely, and gently, inform the sponsor, to help ensure the promotion is run fairly.

How to Deal with Sweeping Addictions

Sweepstaking can be a lot of fun, especially when you win prizes. But if you aren't careful, it can become an addiction.

Following are some points on how to recognize that, and how to counteract the addiction and keep things fun.

Winning can be quite a rush. <u>It's personal validation</u> – validation that all the countless hours you spent entering are finally producing results. <u>It's an accomplishment.</u> It makes you feel good. The first few times you win a prize, your significant other, your family members, your friends, might be really excited for you. <u>And you get a lot of attention.</u> Very quickly though, that rush subsides, and then you want to get the next rush.

If you aren't careful though, it can become a bit of an addiction. You might start entering more, spending more hours in front of the computer to the exclusion of your family members. You might find you even start ignoring them. You might get upset if they don't appreciate the time and effort you put into winning a certain prize. You might find yourself getting up earlier, or staying up later, and forgetting to eat. You might even forget to shower, forget to change, or something along those lines. If you start doing that, it's important to recognize that you may be starting to become addicted to entering sweepstakes. And then it's not the fun hobby that used to be.

How to prevent a Sweepstakes Addiction:

1. <u>Set a specific time you will enter sweepstakes</u>. Nothing more, nothing less. And be satisfied with the amount of sweepstakes you enter. In the same way -- if you started watching 10 hours of TV a day, or started eating 10 meals a day, or played computer games 10 hours a

day – you would recognize that as an addiction, and try and change it. Similarly, if you find yourself entering too many sweepstakes to the exclusion of everything else, then you need to stick to a schedule.

2. Do other activities in your day. You need to have a balance in your life. Go for a walk with your spouse, or play with your children. Go for a drive. Call up a friend for coffee. Go to your local university or college and listen to a lecture. It will help break up your day, and make you feel that you've accomplished something. There is an expression which is very true – "All work and no play makes Jack a dull boy". If you do 'nothing' but enter sweepstakes all day, you can end up with a very stressful life.

3. Find out how to enter more, in less time. I've personally gotten addicted to some activities when they produce results, and then forgotten that there might be a *better* way of doing the same thing. The expression 'work smarter, not harder' is very true. Would you use a butter knife or an axe to chop wood? While I suppose you 'could' chop wood with a butter knife, it would probably take a very long time.

Likewise, tools exist to help you enter more sweepstakes, in less time, and produce the exact same results. You could use a form filler, like Google Auto-Fill, and Roboform, or you can use more specialized Sweepstaking tools designed for sweepstakes like

SweepersChoice to help you enter hundreds of sweepstakes in minutes, not hours.

I'll share an interesting story. When I was a teenager, I was doing some contract work for a company. It was a lot of manual work, and I was being paid a fixed price. They started giving me more and more of this type work. Initially, I just kept doing it the 'manual' way, and tried doing it 'faster', but found it was taking me a very long time and I was getting tired of it. I ended up getting paid very little for the amount of work I was actually doing. But then, I decided to take about an hour out of my own time to figure out how to do it 'smarter'. Finally, I did. Future work ended up taking me about $1/10^{th}$ of the time to complete. I still got paid the same amount, but now I could 'enjoy' the free time I had to pursue other activities, and I still got paid the same amount!

4. Take a break from your activities. I know sometimes this is really hard, but sometimes taking a step back and taking a few days or a week off can help you put things back in perspective. Of course, you don't have to give it up. But just take a break to re-energize yourself.

9. For Companies: How to Run a Successful Sweepstakes

That is, successfully run a sweepstakes that produces _results_.

This chapter is designed for someone that works for a company that wishes to sponsor a sweepstakes, or, if perhaps you wish to win a prize from a company that does not yet sponsor a sweepstakes, you can send them this section. SweepersChoice (http://www.sweeperschoice.com/) has literally worked with hundreds of companies that have run successful promotions, and these are some of the things that we do to help ensure they run them successfully – and run more in the future!.

This section will discuss the benefits, and give you a solid understanding of how to run a successful promotion. It will help give an idea of how to lay some of the groundwork for setting up a successful promotion.

If you just want to enter to win prizes, then this will help give you an 'insight' as to why companies run promotions. If you understand this, and can help the companies achieve their goals, then you can also help yourself increase your chances of winning. For example, you could offer to promote a company promotion to your own Facebook friends in exchange for a small prize.

Benefits of Sponsoring a Sweepstakes

Done correctly, sponsoring a sweepstakes gives you the following direct benefits:

- **Cost effective means of advertising for your company.** You make more sales long-term through word-of-mouth advertising than you spend in prizes and the promotion.

- **Create immense goodwill towards your company.** When consumers think of your company, they associate it with the excitement they felt at winning prizes.

- **Create 'presence of mind' purchase decisions for your products.** It is a known fact (through various psychological studies) that consumers are more likely to make a purchase from a company that they are familiar with, than one that they know nothing about.

- **Increase loyalty and customer fan base.** People like getting involved with companies that offer prizes!

- **Incredible word of mouth advertising.** People will talk about your companies in places you never dreamed of. For example, Castrol USA was sponsoring a sweepstakes to give someone the chance at being a USA soccer correspondent. Not only did one of the entrants talk to a crowd of hundreds of people to get 'votes' at a recent sweepstakes convention that I attended, but I mentioned it in my newsletter to 10,000+ people, asking people to support him, and I am writing about it in a book as well. Where else can you get advertising like that?

Types of Prizes to Offer

This is something that obviously depends on your budget, but I recommend starting out with something small, then growing bigger from there. The first couple promotions you run – you may not see any 'immediate' return. However, as you test, tweak and track the promotions, you will find what works for you and your company. You can then run bigger and larger promotions as you measure the effectiveness of them.

Prize wise, this is what I recommend (in order of value):

- Gift cards, usually with a value of at least $25
- Free products/services, related to your company
- Larger ticket items, like electronics. Right now things such as iPads, e-readers (Kindle, Nook, etc.), laptop computers, big-screen HD TV's, etc are very popular
- Cash prizes. $250, $500 and more work quite well.
- And finally, if you have the budget, really large prizes such as vacations, cars, houses, large cash prizes, plus much more.

Setting Up the Promotion:

To set up a promotion, you must have the following as a bare minimum. I recommend speaking with a professional to make sure everything is included, but this is the bare minimum:

You must have rules for the promotion. Generally speaking, this includes the following:

- A start/end date for the promotion, and entry frequencies (i.e., daily, monthly, one-time, etc)

- Who is eligible to enter (i.e., certain states/provinces/age restrictions)

- The prizes being offered, and their approximate retail value, and total retail value

- A FREE method of entry ('No purchase necessary' method). It is 'okay' to ask for (essentially) a paid method of entry – as long as entrants can also enter for free. Some companies will ask entrants to provide a UPC symbol, product code, etc., but if the entrant does not have this, they can then mail in for a free game piece/UPC symbol/etc that requires no purchase.

- If you do not have a 'free' method of entry, then you need to make it a "contest" that requires 'skill' to win. (I.e., writing an essay that is *judged* based on quality, submitting photographs that are *judged* based on quality, etc.). This is no longer a sweepstakes, it is a 'contest'. If you do not have a free method of entry AND you do not have it as a skill based "contest", then in

most places it becomes a 'lottery'. In that case, most places require you get a lottery license.
- In some jurisdictions, you may need to specify the odds of winning a particular promotion. (I.e., '1 in 10,000 chance', etc.

- How the winner will be selected. Is it a random drawing? Computer drawing? Skill-based selection? You need to specify that.

- Other rules – this may include things such as how a user may be disqualified, special requirements for entering (write an essay, etc), and so forth.

Other beneficial items (but not necessarily required) include having a 3rd party company 'audit' the sweepstakes, to ensure everything is run smoothly and 'fairly'. With a large userbase, this can be a good selling point to get more participation from 'new' users.

Other things to consider:

- If you plan on using the winner's name, photograph and so forth in promotional materials, have the winner sign an affidavit giving you permission to do that. While, of course, you can have that as a stipulation in the contest rules as a term of participation, I still recommend obtaining an affidavit just to be on the 'safe' side.

- If the sweepstakes is extended to Canada, then the (potential) winner needs to respond to a 'skill testing question' to accept the prize. This tends to be a simple math question utilizing all four operators (+ - x ÷). Also, please note, in Canada, "contest" means pretty much exactly the same thing as "sweepstakes" in the USA; meaning a free 'ballot' type entry to win a prize.

- If the sweepstakes is extended to Canada, you will probably want to exclude Quebec. This is because Quebec has its own set of rules regarding how sweepstakes can be run, and it can become very complicated to administer.

- 1099 forms. If the prize you are offering is $600 or over, you need to send the individual a 1099 form for tax purposes.

What is the Purpose of Your Promotion?

Reaching as Many People as Possible?

If the purpose of your promotion is to reach as many people as possible, then I recommend making it as <u>easy</u> as possible for someone to enter, and making it a daily entry. I also recommend having computer programming in place that allows entrants to get 'bonus' entries by referring friends.

If you start requiring CAPTCHAs, membership signups, short essays/surveys/etc and so forth, then you significantly reduce the number of people who will take the time to enter, because it is too much 'work'. (As an aside, CAPTCHAs in reality are not necessary. They are just the 'lazy' man's security method. You can do everything you need to do to help prevent manipulation of a sweepstakes from a backend standpoint without the use of CAPTCHAs. (Backend means the computer programming to accept and analyze entries on the company computer servers). But it is a lot more 'work' to do it correctly 'programming' wise, so that is why most people and/or companies don't.

Marketing Intelligence?

If you want to get 'marketing' intelligence, then obviously including a survey makes sense. However, multiple choice type questions tend to work better. I.e., if you said "How much would you be willing to pay for this product? Fill in the blank: _____", versus "(a) $25-$50, (b) $50-$75, (c) $75-$100", the latter tends to be much more effective, and get a much higher (and accurate) response rate.

I recommend using some 'primer' questions to make sure the data you are obtaining is valid. Sometimes people will just fill in 'random' information just to get an entry, which results in useless marketing data.

For example, I know of a restaurant chain that uses several 'primer' questions to determine which data is valid and which is not. After purchasing a meal, you can get a "free coupon" by entering a survey. It first asks you the receipt number, then which day of the week you made your purchase and at what time. If you choose the incorrect date/time, then it can automatically 'disqualify' this information because it knows that the information is inaccurate. Therefore, it deduces that because you are not taking the time to seriously enter the survey, probably the rest of the information is inaccurate.

Likewise, if you are doing an online survey, you can ask them what state they are entering from. When the data is submitted, do a reverse-IP address lookup. If the state does not match the one they entered, then it is possible that the data they are submitting is not accurate. Then, you could discard the survey results from the main results.

Marketing Materials Creation? ("Crowd Sourcing"?)

If you want people to 'develop' materials for you for free, then using videos, essays, and so forth as a condition of entry is okay. The flipside is that you will have to do a lot of initial promotional work to get people to enter.

For example, as mentioned previously in this book, for the last few years, Doritos has consistently run an annual promotion where they give away $250,000 for people to create mini-commercials (videos) to promote their products. While the number of entrants (relative to the prize value) is quite low – they can literally get hundreds to thousands of free, quality "commercials" for a fraction of the cost that they might pay a professional studio. Plus, as a bonus, those creators tend to share their creations with other users, resulting in very good word-of-mouth advertising. Several years ago, when Doritos first came out with this promotion offering $250,000, they "only" had about 700 video entrants. (Compare this to say another type of sweepstakes that might generate tens of thousands of entrants for a $250,000 cash prize). But, they now had 700 "mini-commercials" that could be shared with friends and family via social properties. This works out to roughly $333 per commercial. Where else can you find prices like that?

If you choose to do a 'crowd' sourcing type of sweepstakes, you will need to do some heavy 'front-end' promotion to get your promotion in front of other people. Sometimes it will 'take-off' right away, and in other cases it won't. So you need to be prepared.

Strengthen Your Core Userbase?

If the purpose is to strengthen your core userbase; i.e., getting people entering regularly and visiting your website, and viewing your products and services regularly, then I'd recommend a 'membership' type of website. (i.e., enter a name/e-mail/confirm the e-mail/etc).

A small caveat. Make sure you run a lot of promotions, and consistent promotions if you want to do this. Coca Cola (mycokerewards.com) does an excellent job of this. I've seen some other companies though that are only running a one-time promotion, but require users to jump through hoops before being able to enter. And they have difficulty with seeing any kind of 'good' results.

If you don't have any kind of effective backend system in place (i.e., rewards programs, bonuses, tell-a-friend type promotions, etc.) – then there is really no purpose to having a membership type of sweepstakes. If, however, you do, then this is an excellent way of increasing 'stickiness' to your site, and long-term fan loyalty.

Third Party Services for Sweepstakes Promotion

There are a number of third party services that help you "create" the promotion. It is <u>not</u> the actual promotion, it is just <u>creating</u> it. (**IMPORTANT NOTE: MOST SERVICES DO NOT ACTUALLY PROMOTE/MARKET THE PROMOTION FOR YOU. THEY JUST MAKE THE 'CREATIVES'. YOU NEED TO DO THE WORK AND PROMOTE YOUR SWEEPSTAKES.**)

That is really important to note. Some companies create promotions, expecting to get thousands of entrants overnight, but are shocked when maybe only 3 or 4 people enter, or, just several people from their existing userbase. I will discuss how to promote effectively very soon.

In the meantime, here are some of the more popular promotional 'creation' services:

-    Wildfire (recently acquired by Google)
-    Woobox

- Offerpop
- NorthSocial
- Shortstack
- Etc, etc.

There are actually literally hundreds of companies offering 'promotional' services, but the above tend to be larger ones.

It's important to note that this list is constantly changing with technology. A lot of the companies on this list didn't even exist several years ago, and just have had a lot of venture capital (VC) funding. So, it's important to do your homework and find the company that helps you to produce the results you want.

To actually run the promotions and do some promotions, you'd be looking at paying a lot more. Some of the companies that do this to some extent (but are very pricey, and results vary) include companies like EPrize (a $70 million year company), and Prizelogic. EPrize recently went on a spending spree acquiring a number of other companies, so that's part of the reason I am not including a few other names here that I otherwise would have.

How Promote Your Sweepstakes

Just because you have an amazing sweepstakes with amazing prizes, does not mean you will get thousands upon thousands of people lining up at your door.

In fact, I've seen many companies offer cash prizes upwards of $10,000, only to have several hundred entrants, if that. And from a company standpoint, I understand why they don't understand why more people wouldn't enter. If no one knows about it, how can they? Getting people to actually take action can be a lot of work.

As I mentioned before, a few months ago I came across the Heinz 57 ketchup promotion. They were giving away $25,000 and only required a photograph uploaded to Instagram. Three weeks into the promotion, with only one week left, they only had about 50 pictures submitted. I'm guessing that equated to 10 entrants. TEN entrants! For $25,000!!! I sent out an e-mail to my newsletter, and within several days this number jumped to 350 pictures submitted, SEVEN times what Heinz had originally.

So, just because you have an amazing prize that you are giving away, does not mean people will enter. You still have to do the promotion of your sweepstakes to get entrants.

Short-Term Promotional Strategy:

Here is how you do it for a 'one-time' (infrequent) promotions. I've prioritized this list in terms of desirability:

1. Promote to your existing list. If you don't already have a newsletter, you should get one. If you do, promote to that and let your existing users know about it. Also, promote to your existing customer base. They are familiar with your products and services, and if they like

it, will most likely tell friends and family, as well as enter themselves.

2. <u>Pay to promote to an existing 'sweepstakes' list.</u> Many sweepstakes sites have thousands, to tens of thousands of eager readers. For several hundred dollars, you can usually get the word out about your promotion easily and effectively. (For example, we have a list of 10,000+ newsletter subscribers that want to learn more about up & coming good sweepstakes promotions).

3. <u>Promote via sweepstakes directories, contest sites, and so forth.</u> Many tend to be free, while others have a nominal fee to get front page ranking.

4. <u>Promote via other social properties.</u> This includes Facebook, Twitter, the up & coming Pinterest, trade related website forums, and so forth. You may also cross-promote with other complimentary businesses within your sector.

5. <u>Include some kind of referral based system.</u> For example, refer a friend and get 3 bonus entries. This helps to introduce 'new' people to the sweepstakes. Also, realize that although some people do nothing but enter sweepstakes all day (called "sweepers"), they can be your best sweepstakes ambassadors. <u>They</u> are the people that are willing to jump through hoops in order to get bonus entries, to increase their chances of winning. "Regular" people don't tend to do that –

because it takes too much 'time'. But sweepers will. So treat them well, and give them opportunities to spread the word.

6. Paid advertising. You need to do your homework and find a company that has a complementary product, and negotiate a deal to advertise on their website for a fixed amount. I do not recommend using PPC (pay per click) advertising when you first start out, because it is very expensive, very competitive, and very difficult to see results unless you know exactly what you are doing. (In some cases, I'd say it's a 'safe' bet that you'd have a better chance of winning a jackpot by playing slots at a casino than getting any significant value with pay per click). This is simply because most people don't know what they are doing, don't know how to compose a proper advertisement, do not understand what 'conversion' rates are, etc. – and so lose their shirt with Google or Facebook advertisements.

7. Use an existing promotional agency. Some tend to be very expensive, and results vary. So, you need to do your homework to find a good one to match your sweepstakes. Starting off 'small' tends to start in the thousands of dollars. I would not recommend looking at this method unless you are prepared to make a long-term investment in your sweepstakes.

Long-Term Promotional Strategy:

Ideally, you will put together a longer term promotional strategy that goes for at least six months, if not longer. Three to four consecutive different sweepstakes, utilizing the 'short-term' promotional strategy tend to work well.

This is simply because it takes a little while to get people 'used' to coming to your website to enter sweepstakes, and/or tell friends through newsletters, website forums, and so forth. However, done correctly, if you consistently have sweepstakes, winners winning, and so forth, you will gradually start to see increased traffic and ultimately, increased sales.

I recommend finding what works best with your audience. Sometimes many prizes with low prize value works well, while other times having one or two big ticket items attracts the attention. I recommend testing both types of sweepstakes to find out what produces results for you.

So, the long term strategy:

1. Hold regular, monthly sweepstakes.
2. Test either having many prizes, low to medium value, or a few big ticket items.
3. Have a smooth process for shipping out prizes.
4. Send prizes via registered mail. (This helps to ensure that prizes are delivered successfully, and it is relatively inexpensive to do so).

5. Promote the winners to your existing fanbase. Pictures of happy people smiling, ideally with their prizes, tends to work out well. (Sometimes you may need to provide a bit of an incentive, such as in the form of an additional free product coupon, to get pictures of winners with their prizes. I recommend setting a time limit of say one week if you choose this method).

Seeing an ROI (Return on Investment)

As with pretty much most companies, the purpose of spending an advertising dollar is to make more than you spend in the long-term.

I recommend the following to help ensure you see results.

Realize that you will probably only start to see results with 3-6 months. For most companies, the purpose of spending an advertising dollar is to make more than you spend in the long-term.

I recommend the following to help ensure you see results.

1. **Realize that you will probably only start to see cumulative results 3-6 months AFTER your promotion has finished.** This is simply because it takes time before other people really start talking about it within website forums, promotional sites, and so forth. If you see some sooner, then that is a bonus.

2. **Sweepstakes Metrics.** Put metrics in place to measure how many people take action. How many people enter your sweepstakes, how many people click on links within your newsletters, and so forth. You want to measure and find out if what you are saying gets people to enter your sweepstakes.

3. **Sales Metrics.** Measure the long-term effectiveness on your bottom line. If you were promoting product 'A' – did you see sales go up? Down? Stay the same? Which of them can be attributed to sweepstakes entrants? Specialized software exists to help you with this type of tracking. You can also develop it in-house.

4. **A/B Split Testing.** This simply refers to testing 'Promotion A' versus 'Promotion B', and seeing which generates the best results. When you figure out which one does, then you *continue* doing testing to find out which tweaks generate the best result, and so forth.

5. **Realize this is an investment, and will require tweaking and testing to produce the best results.** What works for one company may not work for you. Holding a successful sweepstakes is a long-term investment.

And that is pretty much it! If you have further questions about running a successful sweepstakes, or would like SweepersChoice to help you run a successful promotion, you can contact us through our online contact form through http://www.sweeperschoice.com/

10. Conclusion

Entering and winning sweepstakes can be a very exciting hobby. For some, it can even become a full-time job with major benefits. This includes perks such as getting VIP backstage passes to concerts, private lunches with celebrities, around the world tours, plus much more.

For me, it's rather remarkable seeing where I was, and where I am right now.

As I mentioned at the beginning of this book, I remember being a child when our family won a $500 dishwasher. All of us children were really really excited about it. That was because, we (*thought*) we would no longer have to wash the dishes by hand anymore. We could just use the dishwasher. Ironically, at that time, water was really expensive, so it was too expensive to use the dishwasher. We continued to wash the dishes by hand, but just look at that dishwasher in admiration.

Little did I know, that 20 years later, not only would I have software called "SweepersChoice" designed to help save you time, and significantly increase your chances of winning, but also have a book discussing the world of sweepstakes. If you had told me that even five years ago, I probably would've looked at you funny.

But I've learned a lot, met and talked to a lot of interesting people, and I hope that my experiences help you to have a very profitable and enjoyable time with the world of sweepstakes.

One very important thing to remember; it is the companies and the sponsors that make winning sweepstakes possible. So when you win, tell friends and family about the company. Send thank-you notes. Do whatever you can to help promote them. This helps to ensure that there will be even more prizes to win in the future!

That being said, good luck, and start entering!

Johnathan Wyka-Warzecha

11. Future Reading/Movies to Watch

Here are some books & movies that may prove to be useful for you. They may give you some new tips or ideas that you have not heard of before. Others may share interesting winning stories, to help keep you motivated. Many of these books can be found on Amazon.com.

How to Win Lotteries, Sweepstakes, and Contests in the 21st Century

"Successful player and contestant Steve Ledoux shares his skills in choosing lottery numbers, winning sweepstakes and contests, and spotting illegal scams in this savvy collection of prize-winning strategies. Lottery and sweepstakes hopefuls learn how to find the right contests to enter, how to protect themselves from cheaters, and what to expect after winning, including how to deal with the IRS and give interviews to the media. Internet sweepstakes, contests, and resources complete this guide to winning the jackpot." – Book Description from Amazon.com

Contesting: The Name It and Claim It Game, WINeuvers for WISHcraft (Canadian)

"CONTESTING: THE NAME IT AND CLAIM IT GAME How to be a winner--in the contest at your supermarket or in the game of life. Helene Hadsell, who is called "The woman who wins every contest prize she desires," shares her secrets in a manner: vibrant, warm and folksy that is unique to only her. Sample the good life with Helene. She will

cover the secrets for confidence and success and how to visualize your dreams and desires. Learn the nuts and bolts information of contesting mechanics from how to create a winning entry to how to save money on your contesting supplies. Underground Bestseller. Published in both Spanish and Hungarian, the book has sold over 2 Million copies. – Book Description from Amazon.com

The Prize Winner of Defiance, Ohio

Taken from the Amazon.com description, *"The Prize Winner of Defiance, Ohio introduces Evelyn Ryan, an enterprising woman who kept poverty at bay with wit, poetry, and perfect prose during the "contest era" of the 1950s and 1960s. Evelyn's winning ways defied the church, her alcoholic husband, and antiquated views of housewives. To her, flouting convention was a small price to pay when it came to raising her six sons and four daughters.*

Graced with a rare appreciation for life's inherent hilarity, Evelyn turned every financial challenge into an opportunity for fun and profit. The story of this irrepressible woman, whose clever entries are worthy of Erma Bombeck, Dorothy Parker, and Ogden Nash, is told by her daughter Terry with an infectious joy that shows how a winning spirit will always triumph over poverty."

This book was also made into a movie, starring Julianne Moore. Many sweepers have said they have enjoyed both the book & the movie.

12. Glossary of Terms

AVR – Approximate Retail Value. Refers to how much a prize package is worth.

AFFY/Affidavit – An affidavit is a legal document that verifies the information that you submitted is correct and accurate. In some cases, you may need a witness to sign it. Many companies use affidavits to ensure everything is conducted fairly.

Creative Presentation – This means that usually there are a couple or more companies participating in a prize giveaway. For example, the prize might be a car, but there might be 'five' different companies all sponsoring the sweepstakes, with their own separate entry forms. Why this is important to note, is because the odds of you winning may be lower if there are many entrants from different sources.

DOB – Date of Birth. Used on entry forms.

FMV – Fair Market Value. Used to refer to what the 'fair' value of a prize is.

JA/Judging Agency – A judging agency (also known as a 'JA') is a company that administers either part of, or the entire sweepstakes. Judging agencies tend to be used to help conduct fair drawings, as well as bring technical expertise to the table to conduct the sweepstakes.

Contest – In the USA, a 'contest' tends to be like a sweepstakes, but requires an element of skill to win. This may include writing an essay, creating a video, or something along those lines. In

Canada, 'contest' means a free 'ballot' type of entry (virtually identical to the definition of a sweepstakes in the USA).

PIN Code – Personal Identification Number Code. Companies may require that you use a special code in order to participate in their sweepstakes.

Sweepstakes – In the USA, a sweepstakes means a ballot type of entry to win a prize, with no purchase necessary.

SASE – Self Addressed Stamped Envelope. Some sweepstakes require PIN codes to participate. To comply with the 'no purchase' requirement of holding a sweepstakes, if you do not have a PIN, you may send an envelope in the mail to receive a free PIN code to use to enter the sweepstakes. They then send the "SASE" to you with the PIN code.

Short Code – Short codes are 5-digit numbers associated with text message/mobile sweepstakes. In many instances, you will see something like 'Text WINME to #11111'. The number '#11111' would be an example of a short code.

UPC Code/PIN Codes – UPCs (Universal Product Codes) are the bar codes you find on many products in stores. Some sweepstakes may require you to enter a UPC symbol as either a proof of purchase, or at the very least having seen the product. PIN Codes are similar, however tend to be explicitly for the purpose of entering sweepstakes. Coca Cola is well known for their use of PIN codes, and and their rewards program, found on http://www.mycokerewards.com/

USPS – United States Postal Service

Bonus Sweepstakes! How to win EXTRA prizes!

Of course – what would a sweepstakes book be all about, without of course having a sweepstakes surrounding the book?

Go to:

http://www.sweeperschoice.com/bookbonus.php

For your chance to win a cool bonus prize! Winners are randomly selected once a month, and you could be next! Find out how YOU can have a chance at winning some AMAZING bonus cash & other prizes, just for going to that link and following the instructions there!

SWEEPSTAKES MILLIONAIRE!
BOOK ORDER FORM

Did you enjoy "Sweepstakes MILLIONAIRE!", and would like to get a copy for your friends, family, library, sweeping club, or use one for a sweepstakes promotion? "Sweepstakes MILLIONAIRE" makes a great gift for those special winners in your life!

To order online, please go to one of the website URLs located in the bottom right hand corner of this page. Simply select the quantity you wish to order, your shipping information, and then click the purchase button.

If you wish to purchase books in quantities of 25 or more, for your sweepstakes club, library, bookstore or academic institution, special bulk discounts may be available.

For more details, please contact us using our online contact form at:
http://sweeperschoice.com/contact.php

ORDER ONLINE

On Amazon.com
http://amzn.com/1492174610